From Exile to Freedom
Historical Memoir of the Rodzinka Family

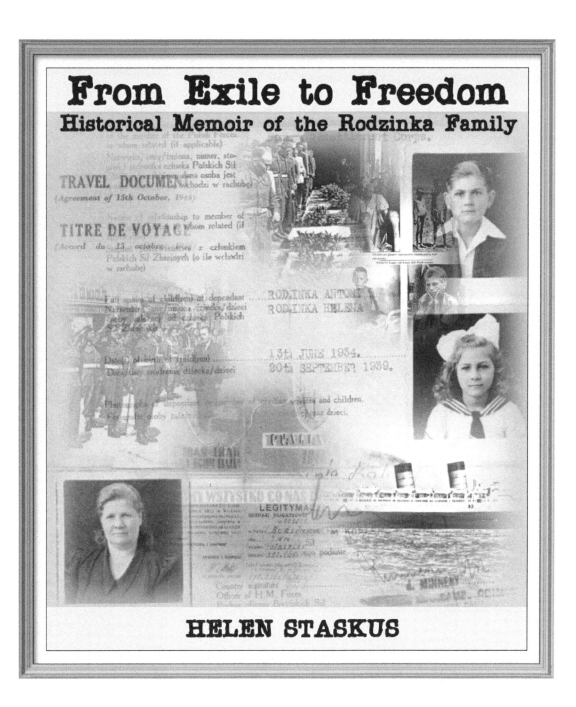

HELEN STASKUS

Cover Design by:
Shelley Brienza of Evolve Today Self–Publishing

Dedication

This story is dedicated to Katarzyna (Grzasko) Rodzinka, our mother. She loved us deeply and hurt deeply when any one of us was separated from her. From 1939 to 1962, we never were a complete family. Yet she did everything possible to search for us when we were not with her and to take care of us (when we were separated) as best she could. Mom was never happy until her whole family came together in America. We thank God for Mom's physical, mental, emotional, and spiritual stability which kept us all strong.

We thank her for her fortitude to hold on to all our documents even through the harshest times. We are blessed to have them. They enhance our ability to understand the lives and the times that we lived through.

Thank you, Mom, for your grace to believe we would all be together and for the struggle you had to make this miracle happen.

Thank you, Mom, for the love you bestowed on us which taught us to love deeply and honestly.

Thank you, Mom, for your generous life and spirit which enables us to give generously to others so they can see the spirit that you bequeathed to us.
Thank you, Mom, most of all for your faith in God during such terrible hard times because you have given us the faith and belief that God is with us in every moment of our life, helping us, providing for us, and showing us there is a way out and leading us to a new life with safety, security, and healing for all our family. Always Remember: The light at the end of the tunnel is God.

Evolve Today Publishing
Shelley Brienza
Mayfield, NY
Email: sdigestpublishing@gmail.com

July 2021
Mayfield, NY
Printed in the U.S.A.

Jan Rodzinka
Hereford England
1949

Katarzyna Rodzinka
Utica, New York
1958

From Exile to Freedom

Historical Memoir of the Rodzinka Family

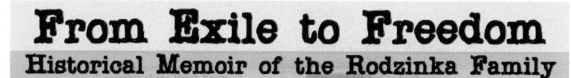

HELEN STASKUS

POLAND

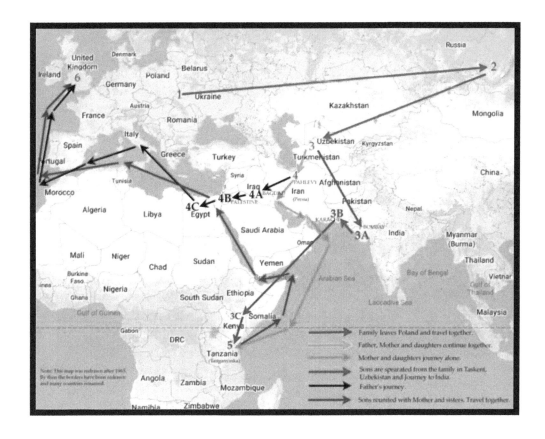

Colony - People of Zmysłow
County Rudki
State - Lwów - POLAND
June 1939
Katarzyna (mom) Stanisław, Janina,
Zofia, Zdzisław & Antoni

MAGDALENA (MOSKAL) GRZASKO w/
grandson: EDWARD GRZASKO - WIKTORIA'S SON
MICHAL GRZASKO
KATARZYNA GRZASKO RODZINKA'S PARENTS
POLAND EUROPE

ALL ELEMENTARY STUDENTS
Teacher: HELENA HABALOWSKA
Imystów — POLAND
Janina, Zofia & Zdzisław Rodzinka

Our Dad: JAN RODZINKA - standing-right
Father Sienkiewicz
Zmyslow   ~ POLAND   1935?

LEONKA (daughter); Karolina
(Dads sister); Felix (Brother
in law); Katarzyna (Dads
mom) & Helena (daughter)
1953? - Brooklyn, N.Y.

FRANEK - JAN - his daughter (CHARISE
GAJASKO. MARYSIA (GRZASKO)
WYKA. KATARZYNA'S SYBLINGS.
probably - HAMTRAMCK - DETROIT - U.S.A

1939 POLAND
Monar sisters
Amiala
Wiktoria &
Franciszka

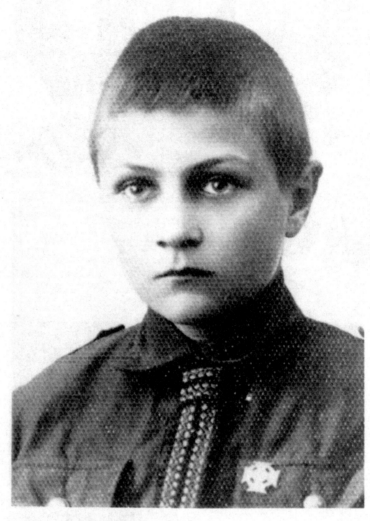

STANISŁAW RODZINKA
13 APR 1923 - POLAND
26 JULY 1942 - WREWSK UZBEKISTAN-USSR

THE RODZINKA FAMILY HISTORY

Our Grandparents—Mom's Side (KATARZYNA)

Father: MIHAL GRZASKO

Mother: MAGDALENA (Moskal) GRZASKO

9 Children:

1. Franek Grzasko-emigrated to the U.S. after W.W. I

2. Jan Grzasko-emigrated to U.S. after W.W. I—Wife-Agnes

3. Katarzyna (Grzasko) Rodzinka

4. Aniela Grzasko Lopusiewicz   (Antoni-husband)

5. Wiktoria Grzasko

6. Franciszka Grzasko

7. Maria (Grzasko) Wyka-emigrated to U.S. after W.W. I

8. Jadwiga Grzasko

9. Stanislaw Grzasko   (Stanislawa-wife)

Our Grandparents–Dad's Side (JAN)

Father: Juzef Rodzinka (was in U.S. and died here-October 20, 1929)

Mother: Katarzyna (Decowska) Rodzinka

4 Children:

1. Zofia-died young.

2. Karolina (Rodzinka) Opatka-husband Felix

3. Franciszek Rodzinka

4. Jan Rodzinka

Both Families lived in the same Township, Wolice-Bzesciany.

Occasionally we come across omissions of historical events that were not fully or properly recorded. Therefore, future generations had or presently have, no knowledge of the complete story.

This is true of what befell 1 ½ to 2 million Polish people (including some Jews, Ukrainians, Belorussians, and others) during World War II. This is a story of EXILE to the Soviet Union on the orders of Josef Stalin, and in due time, disbursement of the "remnant of survivors" to many countries throughout the world. And this is my family's history and the encapsulated events that surrounded our lives.

In 1939 my family was living on a small farm in the village of Sambor, near Lwow, in Eastern Poland.

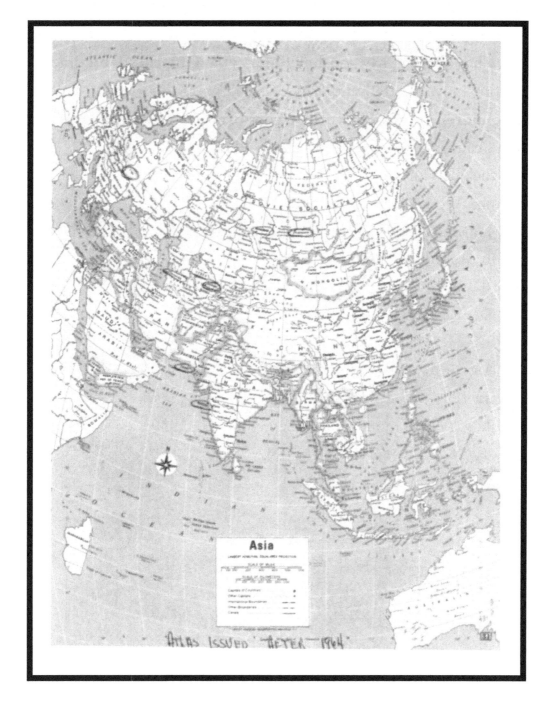

Asia

Atlas issued after 1964

There was my father Jan Rodzinka age 40 (Born–August 13, 1899 and died September 7, 1963); **my mother Katarzyna (Grzasko) Rodzinka age 41** (Born–Nov. 23, 1897 and died Dec. 24, 1981.)

 And six children: (**Ages–The time of deportation to Russia**)

1. Brother Stanislaw Age 16 Born: April 13, 1923

Died in Uzbekistan July 26, 1942

2. Sister Janina Age 12 Born: November 23, 1927

Died: December 26, 2013

3. Sister Zofia Age 10 Born: May 13,1929

Died: June 11, 2013

4. Brother Zdzislaw Age 7 Born March 15, 1932

Died:

5. Brother Antoni Age 5 Born June 9, 1934

Died: August 15, 1994

6. And I, Helena Age 4 months Born: September 20, 1939

Died:

Map: Poland's Borders: 1921 thru 1945
Refer to "Curzon Line"—Border was Changed!

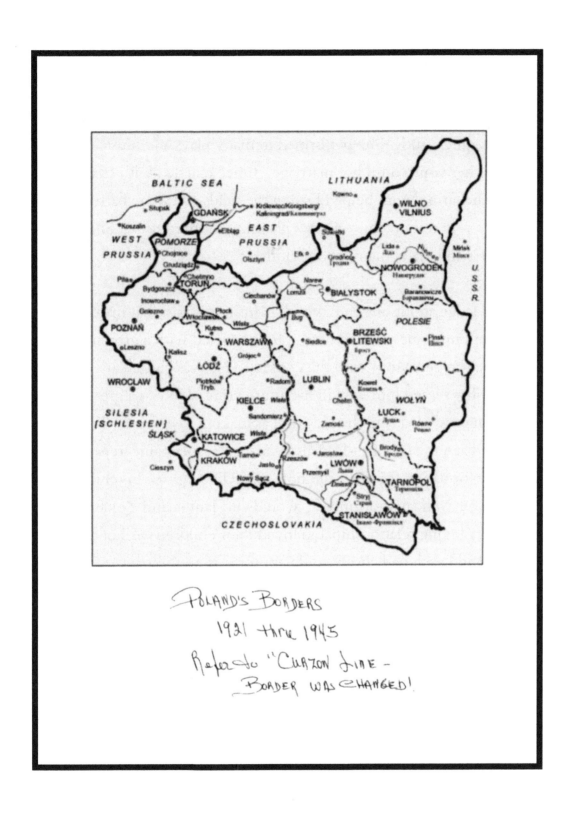

Poland's Borders 1921 thru 1945 Refer to "Curzon Line - Border was Changed!

Our parents were completing the building of our house. They were farmers. We were not well off, but we were not poor because both Mom and Dad had many gifts and talents.

In her youth, Mom, while attending school learned German as well as Russian (Poland at that time was under Austrian rule.) Russian was to be unbelievably valuable in the future for our family, because she had a lovely voice and was a quick study. She performed in many plays and musicals in the village from her youth until her marriage. Once married with children and settled on the farm. Mom helped Dad in the fields and some barn duties. She was very resourceful—always planning for the future. She was a good seamstress and made many of our clothes.

I have no knowledge about our dad's youth. But it was said that my dad pursued my mom until she married him. Once married with a growing family, my father helped Mom with the cooking. He was particularly good at it and that ability served him well in his future years. He was a great craftsman making and repairing shoes as well as making toys for us. For a time, he worked at a toy factory. Dad also was a great mechanic–repairing farm machinery for us and for our neighbors. Dad liked to see his children dressed nicely. On Sunday mornings he would curl Janina and Zofia's hair. My parents had a loving relationship and loved their children. All of them attended school and each had chores to do appropriate to their age. They were good students, but Stanislaw and Janina were exceptional.

See Report Card for Stanislaw from Poland.

7-mio — klasowa Publiczna Szkoła Powszechna

Im. K. W. Jagiełły

w Samborze (powiat: Sambor).

Nr 27 Rok szkolny 1936/37

ŚWIADECTWO SZKOLNE

Rodzinka Stanisław Józef

urodzony dnia 13 Kwietnia 1923 r. w Brzeżanach

(powiat: Sambor), religii (wyznania) rzymskokat.

uczen oddziału siódego otrzymuje za rok szkolny 1936/37

stopnie następujące:

ze sprawowania się . . . . . bardzo dobry   bardzo dobry

z nauki religii . . . . bardzo dobry

"   " języka polskiego . . . . good   dobry

"   " języka ukraińskiego . . . . dobry

"   " języka . . . .

"   " rachunków z geometrią . . . . bardzo dobry

"   " przyrody,   z przyrody żywej   dobry

a mianowicie: z fizyki i chemii . .

z higieny   . . . .

"   " geografii i nauki o Polsce współczesnej . bardzo dobry

"   " historii . . . . bardzo dobry

"   " rysunku . . . . dobry

"   " zajęć praktycznych . . . . . bardzo dobry

"   " śpiewu . . . . bardzo dobry

"   " ćwiczeń cielesnych . . . . . bardzo dobry

"   " robót kobiecych . . . . .

"   " . . . .

Liczba opuszczonych godzin szkolnych 1 , z czego nie usprawiedliwiono 0

Liczba spóźnień 0 , z czego nie usprawiedliwiono 0

Wynik ogólny bardzo dobry

w Samborze , dnia 23 czerwca 1937 r.

Opiekun   oddziału   Kierown   szkoły

Drukarnia Państwowa nr 89781. 10.III.37.   Świadectwo szkolne dla szkół powszechnych 6 i 7-klasowych (P. 1). Cena 8 gr.

But 1939 was the most tumultuous time for Poland as Germany invaded our country on September 1, 1939. Adolph Hitler's Nazi Army already had invaded and captured:

1. Rhineland March 1936
2. Austria March 1938 without a shot being fired.
3. Sudetenland September 1938
4. Slovakia October 1938
5. Monrovia and Bohemia March 1939

After these conquests the Nazi Divisions, two million strong (called Blitzkrieg warfare), attacked Poland from the north, west and the south—marching straight through our entire country. Zdzislaw recalls how the war affected us. He saw German planes flying extremely low over our house and property. When they reached the woods in back of our house, they fired into the wooded area with machine guns to kill any possible hidden Polish soldiers. He says he saw Polish soldiers on horseback who were preparing to fight German tanks. The Germans declared their intention of eliminating the Polish race alongside the Jews.

Within weeks the Polish Army was defeated. The Germans killed the unprepared soldiers taking survivors as prisoners. The Germans destroyed airfields, aircraft, ships, vital communication centers, some railroads, and many cities. When they reached Eastern Poland, they stayed a little while then pulled their army back to the center of Poland.

The Question Arises: Why did they pull out of Eastern Poland? The answer is that eight days before Germany invaded our country they met with Russia and signed the "Ribbentrop-Molotov Pact" on August 23, 1939.

Both of these neighboring countries of Poland would invade, conquer, and partition the Polish Republic between themselves.

Therefore, on September 17, 1939 Stalin's Red Bolshevik Army (The Communists) invaded Eastern Poland. When the Russian Army first came, they smiled and waved as though they were liberators. Soon the smiles disappeared and then they began a reign of terror. The Red Army systematically searched out and arrested all remaining Polish military who had evaded being killed or captured by the Germans. They immediately were labeled as "Rebels" or "Counter Revolutionaries" not as "Prisoners of War."

Poland was now valiantly fighting on two fronts: The Germans on the west and the Russians on the east. Though Poland's military had small victories, it was impossible for them to win. Between 6,000 to 7,000 soldiers died fighting the Red Army. Not only did the Russians round up the military but also the intelligencia i.e., judges, lawyers, physicians, professors as well as police, state employees, business owners and landowners. These were all killed or imprisoned. Torture was used on a wide scale. They were scalded with boiling water, had their extremities cut off, eyes gouged out, and perpetrated even more unbearable horrors. These atrocities took place in the bulging make-shift prisons in Poland. The Russians were second in brutality only to the German Holocaust.

In Western Poland, the Germans declared their intentions of eliminating the Polish race. This process or the "HOLOCAUST" was carried out. They hunted down Polish Military and intelligencia in order to destroy our culture and leadership. Thousands were exterminated at "OSWIENCIM" better known by its German name "AUSCHWITZ" also at "TREBLINKA". On a much larger scale all Polish Jews were herded into "GHETTOS" and then transported to the extermination camps where they were starved, shot, or gassed. The Germans were in the business of exterminating people. On the other hand, the Soviets, while killing many, had other plans in mind. In November 1939, the Soviet government annexed Eastern Poland and declared that 13.5 million Polish citizens were now Soviet citizens. The worst was yet to come.

Many Poles went underground and still others fled the country. Although this act of fleeing our country seems cowardly it turned out to be a Godsend for the Poles in shaping a government in exile for our future lives.

IN DECEMBER 1939: Three months after the Russian invasion our home was robbed. Father was absent visiting his mom and sister in another town. Stanislaw was almost 17 and on patrol duty in the field watching for the Red Army. Mom was in the house with five children when a few invaders broke into our house. She, Janina, and Zofia ran upstairs. Zdzislaw, Antoni and I were asleep downstairs. I, Helena was 2 months old. Mom begged the intruders to take whatever they wanted but not to harm us. Antoni awoke and started crying. The robbers took bedding, warm clothing, and anything of value; but they did no harm to us all. Winter was upon us, and we were in need of warm clothing, bedding and other necessities. My parents decided to send my sister Janina to live with my mother's sister, Aniela and her husband Antoni Lopusiewicz in the city Sambor. Likewise, Antoni was sent to father's sister Karolina and husband Felix Opalka who lived in the village called Medyka.

My sister and brother's stay with family members was to be temporary until our family recovered from the lack inflicted on us by the robbers.

Unfortunately, they never returned home due to the following circumstances:

In February 1940 armed Russian soldiers forcibly entered our home in the middle of the night. Father and Stanislaw were shoved against the wall and were restrained. They searched our house for arms. Finding none, they ordered everyone to get dressed and to pack a few things to take with us. They said that we were "Going to a better place." The frightened children were crying, as the six of us (minus Janina and Antoni) were taken by sled to a train station.

Alas, there were hundreds of frightened families, just like us, already there. When the trains came, we were forced to get into box cars (cattle cars). (See picture of Trains Headed to Russia.)

Illustration by Telesfor Sobierajski is taken from his own story, one of many included in "Stalin's Ethnic Cleansing."

RUSSIA

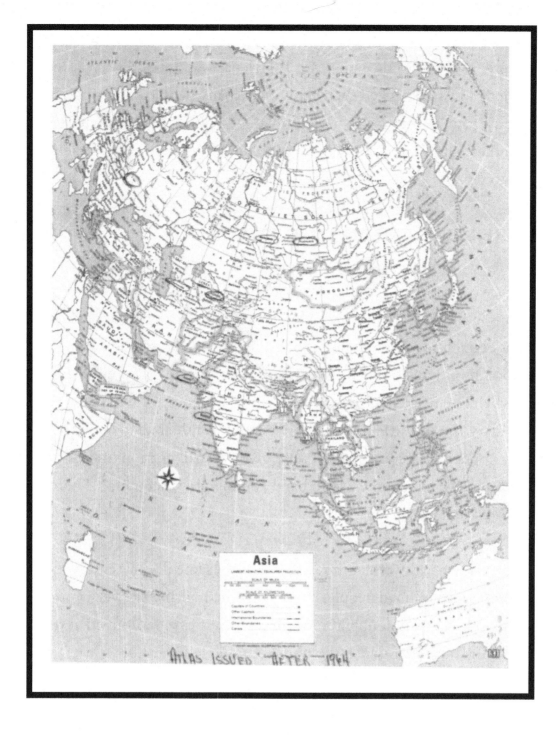

Asia

ATLAS ISSUED AFTER 1964

In all the confusion many families were separated. My family was fortunate for we were loaded onto the same car. I, Helena, was 5 months old at this time. The Red Army packed each car with as many people as possible, 50 to 60 per car. Inside each car were some wooden planks covered with hay, a stove in the center, but not much wood to burn, and there was a hole in the floor to serve as a toilet.

WE WERE BEING EXILED TO RUSSIA!!!

The worst was that it was February right in the middle of winter! Conditions inside the car were horrible. Bitter cold, extreme hunger and thirst, not enough room to lie down to rest made for a brutal journey. People took turns lying down to sleep while others stood. There was no privacy when one needed to relieve himself. The anxiety of what the future held for these people drained all strength from their souls and bodies. The train stopped occasionally. We were given a small portion of dark bread and some watered-down soup barely enough to sustain life. There was never enough for all!

Many who were healthy when they left Poland became ill. Dysentery spread among the confined people. Many elderly, frail and the very young died. Their bodies were simply removed from the cars and dumped at the first opportune time after which the train continued onward.

The destination for all aboard these trains was either:

1. Prisons

2. Labor camps known as concentration camps or "Gulogs."

(See Labor Camps map)

Scanned by Julian Plowy from: "The First Guidebook To Prisons and Concentration Camps of The Union of The Soviet Socialist Republics. Author Avraham Shifrin's book contains detail information of individual prisons and concentration camps, some photos and some camp layout drawings. It is a great book.

3. Collective farms known as "Kolhozs" which were scattered throughout Russia proper and her annexed territories.

Poland's exiles became Russia's forced slave laborers! The main provinces for labor camps were Archangelsk, Kazakhstan, Uzbekistan, and the massive expanses of Siberia which is 77% of the total area of Russia. Siberia covers about 10% of all land surface of our world.

At certain stops some box cars were emptied; and the exiles saw what the miserable future held for them. Some people were on the trains for 1 ½ weeks while others up to 1 month. People were dropped off in the middle of a forest and told to build their own shelters while others were dropped off at existing labor camps, yet others at collective farms.

These exiles worked on expanding railroads, new roads, logging, fishing, agriculture, and building factories by making bricks by hand. These factories refined the abundant precious metals and ores that Russia possessed. Workers dug for gold, diamonds, magnesium, lead, zinc, nickel, platinum and much more.

No consideration was given to the weak or women. These had to work alongside the strong men. Many women died leaving children as orphans. Also, many men were separated from their families and taken to work in other camps.

My family was on the train about 1 month. We had traveled about 2,400 miles. Our deportation ended at a labor camp in Krasnoyarski Kraj in Asiatic Siberia. Siberia was labeled as "Gehenna" or as the "Inhumane Land."

(See our labor camp map in USSR)

RUSSIA

Once off the train we went by sled to this labor camp. Thanks be to God
we all survived.

(Refer to Large Map, exhibit one) Follow route from Lwow, Poland (# 1)
to Krasnoyarsk, U.S.S.R (#2)

This small camp named "Parpaja Bieda" was run by a commandant who turned out to be a decent Russian. He lived there with his wife and young son. He was in charge of about 20 families. We lived in poorly constructed barracks. My family of 6 shared a large room with the "Rydel" family of 7.

There was a wood fireplace in the center for heating and cooking. It also served as a dividing line separating living spaces for both families. Wooden planks against the wall covered with straw served as beds.

The camp was located in an expansive coniferous forest. Mom and Dad, Stanislaw, with all old enough to work and that included my sister Zofia were sent to the forest to collect Resin, a sap from pine trees. This Resin was useful for medicines, varnishes etc. The workday was exceptionally long. Workers wore netting over their heads to keep away the swarms of flies from their faces. Zdzislaw recalls that Father, upon returning to the barracks, had icicles hanging from his mustache. All workers were covered with the sticky sap. It was impossible to wash it off as there was no soap. The workers were undernourished and inadequately dressed for the work in the severely cold climate. Also, they did not have ample time to regain their physical strength.

They were paid meager wages in "Rubles." The money was used to purchase dark, heavy bread that was brought in by sled. Zofia recalls that occasionally they brought in dried fish. Mom made sure to ration the portions so that we always had something to eat. Leaving the camp was forbidden, yet Mom would sneak out late at night and walk to a small Russian village to beg for food. Because she spoke Russian, the good-hearted women gave her what they could, a few potatoes, some flour or sauerkraut. Therefore, at times, we were blessed to eat soup. The drink that we all had was called "Kipyatok" which was only hot water. As for the children, they had chores, but they also attended classes to learn Russian so that they would become "good communists." Mom and Dad were prayerful people and our family quietly took refuge in our Lord Jesus Christ.

The conditions in the labor camp were very harsh. Lice were plentiful. Bugs that lived in the wood of the barracks would bite us at night, so we were unable to sleep well. Some of us were sick with dysentery and Typhoid fever. Zofia and I developed "night blindness" due to vitamin deficiency. Adding to all the stress my parents experienced was not knowing what had happened to Janina and Antoni who were left behind in Poland. Zofia recalls that at some point they found out that Janina was alive and living with relatives in Poland. But soon contact was lost again. As for Antoni they were unable to find out what had happened to him. Yet, our family was surviving because father was with us and both my parents were hard working and resourceful. When spring arrived, they found leeks; they cleared a patch of land for a garden and planted potatoes and carrots. Later in the season Zofia and Zdzislaw picked berries and Stanislaw and my parents picked mushrooms.

Not all camps were overseen by a "good commandant" like ours. Therefore, many people died due to excessive hard work, lack of warm clothing, diseases, and starvation.

See Poem by Beata Obertynska:

GULAG, a new government agency administering these camps, came into being. The inmate population increased rapidly to 5 million by 1936, while by 1943 the number tripled or even quadrupled, by some estimates. These deportation places were established in such a way that the labor of prisoners benefited the Soviet Union at the expense of the prisoners' survival. Indeed, these were death camps where people were sent to perish. This aspect of the camps is well expressed by a poem by Beata Obertynska:

```
Supplications
    From hunger,
    From marches,
    From rain,
    From lice,
    From strong wind that slashes your face,
    From fire's warmth-when at night they order you
to leave it,
From marshlike taiga that you sink in up to your knees,
From torn-off shoe soles,
From stolen breadbag-Save us, Lord!
From tundra lying on its back facing the sky,
From nightmare of white nights,
From swarms of mosquitoes,
From sudden and unexpected night marches,
From leaden dawns to sooty dusks,
    --Holy God!
    --Holy Almighty!
    Holy and Immortal, save us, oh Lord!
    We the sinners,
    We the tired,
    We the ones given up to vast expanses,
    We the ones cast out to be eaten alive by the frozen
wastes,
    We the ones deprived of humanity and legal rights,
    Trampled like grass,
    Hounded down and rounded up-
    We the louse-infested beggars,
    We the ones stupefied by hunger,
    We the nameless multitude
Poisoned by wrongdoings,
We the filthy,
We the ragged,
We at times the ludicrous,
We the consoled,
We the sinners,
You Lord God we beg,
The Living and True,
The One and Indivisible,
    --Holy God!
    --Holy Almighty!
    --Holy and Everlasting, have mercy on us!
Through the last,
posthumous
Wound of thy Son
through His Blood and Suffering
    Amen - Amen - Amen (1)
```

Recorded Facts:

In 1940 and 1941 four mass deportations of Poles took place from Eastern Poland to Russia. It also included a small percent of Ukrainians, Jews, and Byelorussians etc. who had lived in Eastern Poland.

1.10 February 1940-250,000 from rural areas sent to Siberia in 110 cattle trains. This was the transport that my family was on.

2.13 April 1940-300,000 mostly women and children sent to Kazakhstan and Altai Kraj on 160 trains.

3. June/ July 1940-400,000 to Arkhangelsk, Sverdlovsk, and Novosibirsk etc.

4.June 1941 280,000 to various parts of the U.S.S.R.

Note: Additionally, the 500,000 military and intelligencia who had been imprisoned in Poland were also deported. They were sent to prison or labor camps. Thousands of military people were executed. Example: Katyn Forest massacre was located near Smolensk. A documentary was made about this tragic event around 12 years ago.

It has been reported that 1.7 million Poles and it has been alleged that as many as two million Poles were in captivity in the Soviet Union. The deportations stopped only because Germany invaded Russia. Hitler broke his pact with Stalin and attacked Russia on July 22, 1941. The invasion was called "Operation Barbarossa." Three million Nazis invaded Russia. By September 1941, Stalin lost 2 ½ million men, 14,000 planes and 18,000 tanks. Germany seemed to be unstoppable with her conquests.

Polish Government:

The Polish Government and military personnel who initially fled Poland for France left that country when it was invaded by Germany. They fled to London, England where they established a "Polish-Government-In-Exile" with W. Radzkiewicz as President and General W. Sikorski as Prime Minister.

Meanwhile, Russia, now under attack by Germany, needed as many allies as it could find. Therefore, with Britain's help, an agreement was signed between the "Polish-Government-In-Exile" and Russia called "Sikorski-Maysky Pact" on July 30, 1941. This agreement was signed in London in the presence of Winston Churchill, England's Prime Minister and Anthony Eden.

And, thanks be to God, the agreement was:
1. The release of the Polish people from labor camps and prisons.
2. From these freed people would be the formation of a Polish Army under the command of General Wladyslaw Anders who was released from Lubyanka Prison in Moscow.

Russia called this Pact "Amnesty", yet the Poles never were guilty of any crimes. Still, this was our hope for freedom, our God given right and for many salvation from certain death. The Amnesty was signed in July 1941, yet this news never reached the great majority of people who were scattered throughout the Soviet Union. This news did not reach many who were in remote camps until Dec. 1941. For others, the news never reached them at all. This was intentional as Stalin led the Allies to believe that all deportees would be freed. Yet, he only allowed approximately 100,000 to be released from prisons and labor camps. Therefore, these Poles were doomed to live out their lives in Russia. All efforts by Sikorski and Anders to obtain release of all failed.

Our camp commander was given authority to let us go free!

Note: These are Zofia's and Zdzislaw's recollections on how we learned about the Amnesty. The camp commander read the Amnesty Proclamation and said that we were free to leave the camp. Everyone rejoiced! My family as well as others gathered all their possessions in bundles on their backs and walked to reach the nearest Russian village. There we met families who were released from other camps. These families were better prepared than we were. They pulled their belongings on two wheeled carts. Father got one for us and this made our walking much easier. Along the way we learned that we needed to reach the city of Novosibirsk. The city had a train station connecting the Trans-Siberian Railroad to major areas of the Soviet Union. We needed to travel South and then south-west. But Novosibirsk was still far away. And Uzbekistan was over 1,000 miles away.

So, from the Russian Village we walked about 20 miles and reached a collective farm. We stayed there from late fall of 1941 through early spring of 1942. Around this time Stanislaw was showing signs that he was not well. Dad and Mom did everything they could to bring him back to health. On this farm Mom went to work digging potatoes and milking cows. Dad worked repairing and running machinery. They earned some money.

We left the collective farm walking and reached Novosibirsk in the spring of 1942. There were hundreds of people, most of them freed Poles from Siberian camps. Father left us sitting on a bench while he went looking for the Polish Government Bureau and was directed to go and buy tickets for us to travel to Uzbekistan (where the army was to be formed.) Also, while there Dad spotted his brother-in-law, Felix Opalka. Felix led all of us to Dad's family who also had been deported from Poland to Siberia. We saw Dad's mother, Katarzyna, his sister, Karolina, her three daughters, Krystyna, Helena, and Leonka, and of course our brother, Antoni. Antoni, at first, was in tears. He did not want to leave his new family; but in a while the tears stopped, and he beamed a smile. We took him with us. What a joyful reunion that was for our family! We were together again with the exception of Janina, who was in Poland.

We boarded the train.

Recollections of our journey south and southwest are sketchy.

The fortunate freed Poles were unsure how to reach these designated areas and by what means. Because they were scattered throughout the huge expanse of the Soviet Union it was impossible to form an organization large enough to help direct thousands to reach the places where the Polish army was being formed. Yet, there sprang up some diplomatic outposts to aid people to reach these destinations.

Once when Dad left the train to obtain food for us the train left the station before he returned. Mom was sure that we would never see him again. Yet, God was merciful to us and sometime later we were reconnected with him. During the time of travel locomotives were changed and prolonged stops were made at major cities such as Barnaul, Semipalatinsk, and Alma-Ata.

After many days of travel, we entered Uzbekistan. The city was Tashkent. We had traveled around 1,500 miles from Siberia.

(Refer to large map follow route from Krasnoyarsk #2 to Tashkent #3)

My parents found work on another collective farm. We lived in a hut. We occupied one side and the other side was occupied by an Uzbek family. They belonged to the Mongolian Race. The main crop grown there was rice. Mom worked in the field and Dad ran and repaired machinery.

Stanislaw's health was quickly deteriorating. After a time, we left the collective farm and headed for the city of Wrewsk. This was our final destination to reach the formation of the Polish Army.

The formation of the Polish Army started in several areas, but it was eventually and permanently moved to Turkmenistan, Kyrgyzstan, and Uzbekistan with its headquarters at Yangi-Yul near the city of Tashkent. Turkmenistan, Kyrgyzstan, and Uzbekistan were three republics out of around 16 that were annexed by the U.S.S.R.

What Happened to Us?:

In Wrewsk near Tashkent organizations were formed to care for the amassed refugees. Posts were formed to enlist able bodied men and women into the army. Dad left to enlist in the army. He took Stanislaw with him who was now extremely sick. Stanislaw enlisted in the "Junaki", (Reserve Cadet of Officers.) He endured one week of training and was declared too sick to continue with training and was sent to a make-shift army hospital. My parents were hopeful that at that hospital he would be brought back to health.

To protect the remainder of the children from the elements, Mom placed Zofia into a girls' organization; Zdzislaw and Antoni into an orphanage, one appropriate for their age and I, Helena age 3, placed into another orphanage. We were all in different locations, but we had a roof over our heads and a little food. Mom on the other hand, with the rest of the older women and men had no place to stay but had to sleep outside.
In the morning and throughout the day she would visit each of us to see how we were doing. She spent most of her time at the hospital encouraging Stanislaw with the hope that he would get better.

Family Split:
Once again, for the second time, the following circumstances split our family apart. Without my parent's knowledge Zdzislaw and Antoni's orphanage was shipped out to India.

At this point we leave our story in Uzbekistan and follow the story of Zdzislaw and Antoni and their travel and life in India.

INDIA

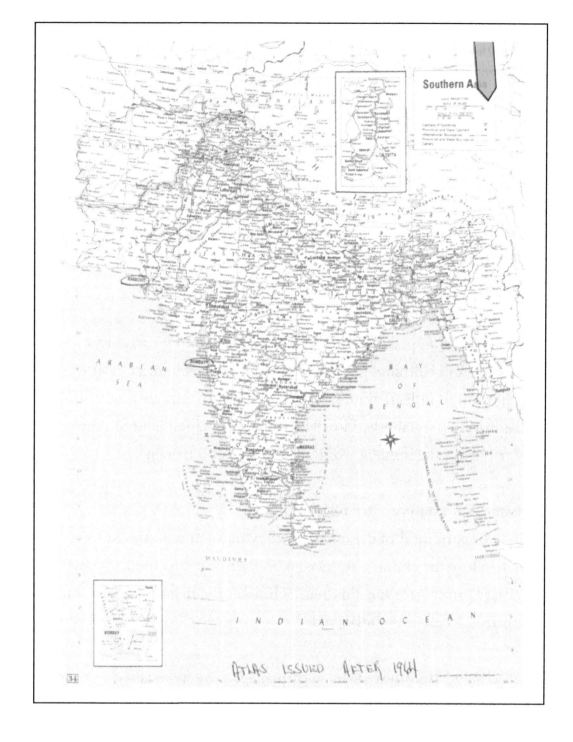

Southern A[...]

ATLAS ISSUED AFTER 1964

INDIA: Zdzislaw and Antoni's Story—

News reached India that thousands of orphaned Polish children were undernourished, sick and many dying in the Asiatic Southern Provinces of Russia. The angered Polish settlers in Bombay, India undertook relief action. They gathered support from the Indian Princely State (which was separate from British India) and their Council was headed by Maharaja Jam –Saheb. With financial support from them and other affluent groups they with the Polish Colony and the Red Cross organized a relief expedition from Bombay to Tashkent.

They left on well equipped, heavy trucks driven by Hindus carrying medicine, food, and clothing. The journey was long and difficult. It took them north through India (Pakistan did not come into existence until 1948), through Afghanistan (established in 1919–which remained neutral during World War II from the influence of Russia, U.S., and Britain.)

This humanitarian transport arrived in Tashkent. When they saw the extremely poor condition of the children, they pleaded with the Soviet Authority to allow the children to leave with them back to India. They secured "Exit Permits" for the children. This was the first rescue operation that took place. Many more followed.

Since Zdzislaw and Antoni were in an orphanage they were taken to India. Unfortunately, my parents were not aware that this took place. When they found out they were extremely sorrowful that once again our family was split apart. Zdzislaw was 10 and Antoni was not quite 8 years old. Zdzislaw recalls that they traveled very many days in the truck on mostly dangerously narrow roads along rugged mountains. It is estimated that this journey encompassed several thousand kilometers.

(Refer to Large Map which shows the route from Tashkent #3 to Bombay #3A).

They first arrived in Bombay (Now Mumbai), a port city on the Arabian Sea. They lived in the suburb of Bombay in an exceptionally large house surrounded by date palms and regular palm trees. They lived close to the sea and went swimming often. The boys were treated well.

Refer to FIRST map of India.

Locations of places in India!

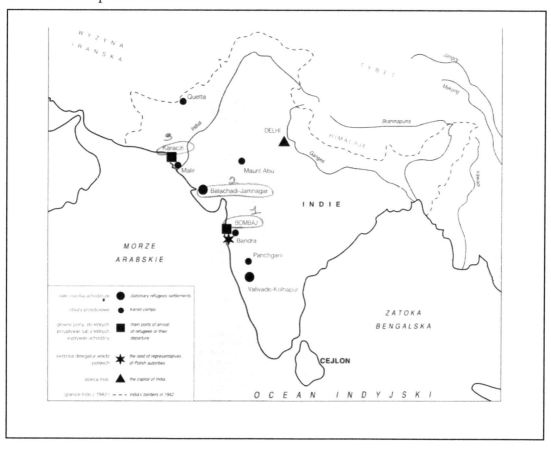

This was a transitional place, therefore after a short stay they were relocated to a permanent camp built in Balachadi near the city of Jamnagar. This site was offered by Prince Saheb at his private seaside resort.

In July 1942, the first group of children and teens arrived in Jamnagar. They with other boys and girls, lived in barracks. Boys and girls were separated and well supervised. All were cleanly dressed, fed, had health evaluations.

By 1946 about a thousand children were there. In 1942/1943 the construction of another settlement started in Valivade near the city of Kolhapur. In June 1943, the first groups of refugees arrived at that settlement. They arrived from Persia. Most of them were women and children. By 1948 about 5,000 people passed through that camp. In spite of the children's poor physical state and hard climate, educational and medical facilities were quickly set up. All of the youths (including my brothers) living in the two camps went to school. At first there were not enough teachers, books, or classes to accommodate the varied ages of the children. But in less than a year, Valivade had three kindergartens, four primary schools, a grammar and secondary school, a trade school and a school that would help adults become teachers. Altogether there were 2500 students, the young, older youths as well as adults were offered good preparation for their future. (Information from the Book: Exiled Children- See Pgs. 80 and 82.)

Cultural activities, youth organizations (i.e., libraries, clubs including scouting) were formed as well as sporting activities. The elder youths went on many outings that exposed them to India's culture and way of life. The younger children also went on some adventures. Zdzislaw recalls when Antoni and their group went to a nearby village and for the first time, they saw beautiful peacocks. Another trip that the boys went on was to see a magnificent Maharaja's palace. Located in the desert, there were many cactus plants growing in the sandy soil. By the palace was a large swimming pool filled with fish. The boys enjoyed swimming in it with the fish!

(See Photo of Maharaja)

stosunkiem do dzieci. Wielkie osiągnięcia organizacyjno-wychowawcze osiedla, obok niewątpliwych zasług całego polskiego personelu, były możliwe dzięki osobistemu zaangażowaniu i niezwykle serdecznemu, niemal ojcowskiemu stosunkowi do dzieci polskich maharadży Jam Saheba. Nie tylko hojnie zasilał wciąż pustawą kasę osiedla, ale też żywo interesował się polską kulturą i sztuką, a do jego ulubionych lektur należeli „Chłopi" Reymonta. Nie opuścił żadnej osiedlowej uroczystości, z wielkim zainteresowaniem oglądał występy naszych zespołów artystycznych, które z reguły zapraszał na ponowne spektakle do swego pałacu w Jamnagarze. Był wielkim entuzjastą sportu, kibicował naszym drużynom rywalizującym z miejscowymi zespołami. W listopadzie 1946 r., gdy z osiedla wyjeżdżała ostatnia grupa dzieci, osobiście

najmłodszych. W naszych sercach pozostanie do końca życia jako niezwykle miły, życzliwy i serdeczny przyjaciel polskich dzieci. Prawdziwie dobry człowiek z „Dobrej Ziemi" jak nazywany jest ten zakątek kontynentu indyjskiego – ziemia jamnagarska.

WIESŁAW STYPUŁA

Maharadża Navanagaru – Jego Wysokość Jam Saheb.
The maharaja of Navanagar, His Highness Jam Saheb

Pałac maharadży Jam Saheba w Jamnagarze 1945 r.
The maharaja Jam Saheb's palace in Jamnagar

Bock: EXILED CHILDREN

It is especially important to say here that all the children including my brothers were treated very well and their caretakers also were exceedingly kind. In comparison to the millions of Hindus that were extremely poor due to the "Caste System" that existed. Although the "Caste System" was outlawed in India, it seems to still be in use. In fact, it seems to have come over to the U.S.

Once again, another move was ahead for my brothers. From Jamnagar, they, and others, were transported to the port city of Karachi. The month and year is unclear. There the children lived in tents. Close by was a British Military Camp. The children saw planes flying by. The most popular game the Brits played was football (American Soccer). Zdzislaw remembers when once they went to the zoo. Other enjoyable times the children had were when the British soldiers hung a sheet on a water tower and the children were treated to movies –in English, of course. Their stay in Karachi was not long. The time came when they boarded a Cargo Ship, once again, not knowing their destination or fate. Young and away from family, we can only imagine the many times that my brothers experienced fright and anxiety!

Their ship sailed on the Arabian Sea. A British ship was zigzagging in front of theirs–sweeping the water for mines placed by Japan. Three days later the ship sailed away. The major countries at war were Japan, Italy, and Germany (called The Axis Powers) who fought against the Allies–U. S., England, and Russia.

In 1948, the last Polish settlement ceased to exist in India. All Polish orphans and adults left that welcoming country and were dispersed all over the world including Mexico. More will be written on this topic later.

While sailing on the cargo ship the boys were confined inside in close quarters and they were only allowed to go on deck in good weather. One time Antoni went up on deck by himself to get some fresh air. The weather was stormy, and he was almost swept overboard. Antoni spoke about this incident many times. From that time, he became cautious when going on deck. The ship sailed on and entered the Indian Ocean; then, we believe, it sailed into the Port of Mombasa, Kenya, Africa. We also think that the children were sent to live at Makindu in Kenya, a transitional camp formed in preparation to reunite separated families, like ours. Children without families would be sent to orphanages set up in permanent settlements throughout Africa. While at that camp my brother vividly recalls how scared they all were when they heard the lions roar each night. Yet, during the day the lions went elsewhere.

The children were poorly taken care of at that camp. They were undernourished. They received some bread and melon once a day. Water was their drink. Gienek Opalka an older boy that they knew from Poland kept some of their bread for them for their evening meal.

Here we leave Zdzislaw and Antoni's Story.

We now resume the story of Dad, Mom, Stanislaw, Zofia, and Helena in Uzbekistan.

UZBEKISTAN

AND

IRAN

Uzbekistan and Iran (called Persia until 1935)

We resume our story in Uzbekistan, a Soviet Socialist Republic. At this time, the three countries that separate our family are:

1.Janina is hopefully safe somewhere in Poland.

2.Zdzislaw and Antoni are somewhere in India.

3.Dad, Mom Stanislaw, Zofia, and I are in the city of Wrewsk near the capital city of Tashkent, Uzbekistan.

This is a place where the Polish Army was forming. To better understand our future the following facts are relevant. When the army was forming, General Wladyslaw Anders was hopeful that they would fight on the German-Russian front. This would open up the road back to entering Poland. He soon found out that Stalin would never relinquish his hold on Poland's land or on the Polish people in Russia. The General realized that his army was to fight the Germans for Russia yet never to be rewarded for any victories they won. It seemed hopeless-there was no way out of Russian bondage for the Poles!

But in July 1942, the British Army suffered a heavy defeat in Africa. This loss threatened Egypt, Iraq, Iran, and the Caucuses, which was called the Middle Eastern front. The Caucuses and northern Iran belonged to Russia. German victories in those areas would be devastating to Russia because these areas were extraordinarily rich in oil. Therefore, Stalin offered Britain (who owned Southern Iran) the help of some Polish divisions to fight German aggression. Stalin agreed that the Anders Army would be used on the Middle Eastern front.

This directive was a blessing for it allowed Anders Army to leave Russian soil for Iran. Additionally, the General issued an order that families of military, including orphans, were also allowed to leave. He stipulated that as many civilians as possible, especially orphans, should be transported from Uzbekistan to the port city of Krasnovodsk (now Turkmenbashy) in the

Russian Republic of Turkmenistan then across the Caspian Sea to the port city of Pahlavi (now Bander-E-Anzali), Iran.

My father was in the Army therefore our family would be scheduled to leave Uzbekistan. But, alas, Stanislaw was extremely ill. Mom was with him in the hospital every day. She prayed and encouraged him that he would get better. But he knew how sick he was, that he would be unable to leave with us when the time came. Stasiu (our special name for him,) told Mom we should not stay behind for his sake. Mom reassured him that she would never leave without him.

It was July 1942. Mom as usual went to the hospital to take care of Stasiu. She found the bed empty and was told that he died that night. Crying she was led to identify his body. When she saw him, she screamed and sobbed! Stasiu's whole body was covered by ants. This wonderful, smart young man, her first born, died at age 19 (July 26,1942.) Dad was allowed to come and see his son. Sorrow upon sorrow! They both grieved! Dad built a wooden box. Stasiu and another young man, with no family, were placed in it and buried. The usual burial of deceased was wrapping them in a sheet and placing one on top of another in the ground. Each time Mom recalled this sad story she had tears well up in her eyes!

Just one week after Stasiu died, Mom was notified to report to the Army Commandant. She was issued a passport for her and me allowing us to depart to Iran.

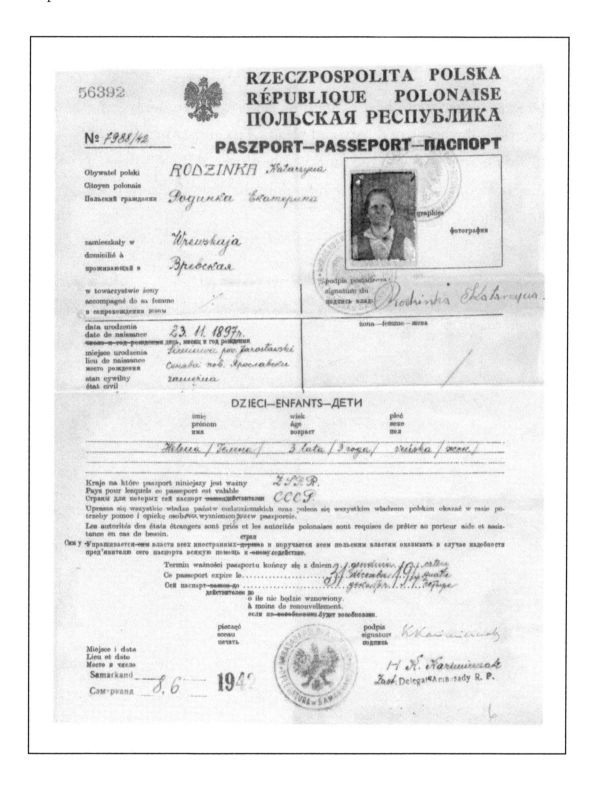

Zofia was still with the Junaki (young woman's organization) and had to travel with that organization.

Mom and I were the first to leave Uzbekistan traveling on the Trans-Siberian Railway to Krasnovodsk. Hundreds were already there sitting on the shore awaiting a ship to take them out of Russian territory. The Kara-Kum Desert was fiery with heat as the sun beat down mercilessly overpowering all who were thirsty and weak. The air permeated with fumes from the refineries and the murky-oily waters of the Caspian Sea discouraged anyone from refreshing himself in the water. (From Book "Stolen childhood" pgs. 66-68.)

Then our ship arrived. A list of names was read. We went aboard a Russian coal ship. It was overcrowded. Every space on board was filled.

Kresy-Siberia Memorial Gallery: Second Evacuation from Krasnovodski, USSR to Pahlevi, Persia (now Iran) in 1942 and later to other places.

The evacuation ships were incredibly overcrowded with thousands of passengers.

Crossing the Caspian Sea, the ship neared Pahlavi, Iran. Everyone wanted to disembark as quickly as possible –to be out of reach of Soviet Authority. (Refer to Large Map —follow route from Tashkent #3 to Krasnovodsk and to Pahlavi #4.)

Upon setting their feet on Iranian soil the people kissed the ground, prayed, cried, and laughed. This was an outpouring of thanksgiving to Jesus, our Lord, that at last they were free!

Mom and I were in Pahlavi. A week later Dad with part of the army arrived. Zofia also arrived on the same ship.

AT LAST WE WERE FREE! BUT AT WHAT PRICE?

Between March 1942 and November 1943, the "EXODUS" took place from Russia. Out of 1 ½ million deportees only 115 thousand Poles (including a few other nationalities) half-starved, some in rags left Russian Soil for Iran.

There were 78 thousand military men including some elderly men and 37 thousand women, their children, and many orphans. Therefore only 7% of Poles were fortunate enough to obtain freedom!

Why did such a small number see freedom?
1. Thousands remained in the Soviet Union not knowing about the "Amnesty".
2. It is estimated that about half of the people died during their actual deportation journey from Poland to Russia.
3. Many exiles died in labor camps due to hard labor, extreme climate, disease caused by epidemics and starvation.
4. After "Amnesty" people died or got lost attempting to reach designated areas.

5. Thousands of imprisoned officers and intelligencia were executed at several forest sites. The first mass graves were discovered recently at Katyn Forest near Smolensk.

I do not fully understand all that took place to the Poles that were deported to the Soviet Union, but more information is coming out regarding the atrocities perpetrated by Stalin on all Slavic nations.

Move to Iran:

The evacuation of Polish Military from USSR took place by sea from Krasnovodsk to Pahlavi and to a lesser extent overland from Ashkhabad, Turkmenistan to Mashhad, Iran.

When the British and Persians were told of the arrival of the Polish Army to Pahlavi a city of 2,000 tents was hastily erected along the Pahlavi Shore. It stretched for several miles. A vast complex of bathhouses, latrines, sleeping quarters, cooking facilities and a hospital were erected. Only a few days earlier they were alerted that in addition to the military---civilian women, their children and orphans would also be arriving. As they watched the refugees leave the Soviet oil tankers and coal ships, they were unprepared to house all of them and were alarmed at the physical state people were in. Especially sad to watch were the orphans who were little more than walking skeletons covered with rags and lice.

See pictures in Pahlevi (Iran) on next page.

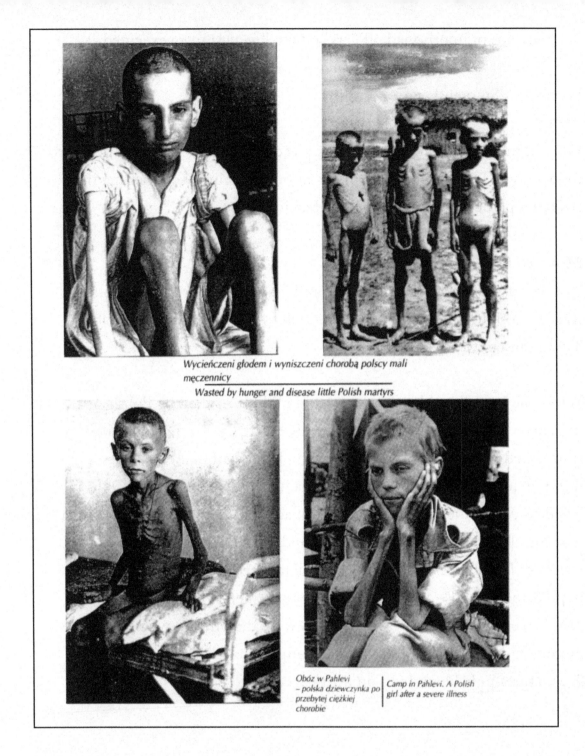

Wycieńczeni głodem i wyniszczeni chorobą polscy mali męczennicy

Wasted by hunger and disease little Polish martyrs

Obóz w Pahlevi – polska dziewczynka po przebytej ciężkiej chorobie | *Camp in Pahlevi. A Polish girl after a severe illness*

After over two years of living in inhumane conditions all were weakened. We were suffering from exhaustion, dysentery, malaria, skin irritations, itching scabs, chicken blindness and typhus. Of most importance was to stop the spread of typhus! There were few doctors and nurses for this enormous mission, but the results were great. The arrivals (we) went through a series of tents; first stripped of clothing which was burned; showered, deloused, many had heads shaved, at the end we were given clothing, sheets and blankets by the International Red Cross and directed to tents to rest. This enormous job was done well. The food served, regrettably, was inappropriate. The rich food of corned beef, fatty soup, lamb, and some bread could not be tolerated by the starved people and a large number died.

Polskie „miasteczko" na piaskach Pahlevi.
Na pierwszym planie charakterystyczne „budowle"
sklecone z żerdzi

Polish „little town" on Pahlevi sands. In the
foreground characteristic „buildings" made from poles

Po przebyciu Morza kaspijskiego pierwszy sen na
wolnej ziemi perskiej. Śmiertelnie zmęczone, ale już
wykąpane i przebrane polskie dzieci odpoczywają
na plaży w Pahlevi

After crossing the Caspian Sea first night on free Persian
soil. Polish children deadly tired, yet already washed
and in fresh clothes resting on the beach in Pahlevi

PAHLAVI - CORRECT NAME
PAHLEVI (POLISH)
IRAN

FROM BOOK
EXILED CHILDREN

EXHIBIT 11 B

Refuges remained in Pahlavi for a few weeks to several months then transported to Teheran, Maszhed, Isfahan (mostly for orphans) and Ahvaz. Because of the weakened condition and epidemics (especially typhus) many more died in each of these camps.

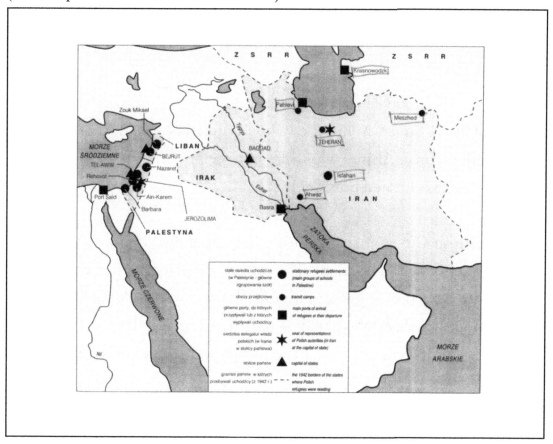

Mom and I were already in Pahlavi a week when Dad and Zofia arrived on the same ship. Dad with the soldiers was sent to a Military Camp. Zofia arrived with the Junaki Organization. She recalls how sandy and hot it was. All went through the tents for cleaning and hygiene. She was in tears when they shaved her head. After a few days she was released into Mom's care. She was incredibly happy to be with Mom. From then on, she helped Mom take care of me. Several weeks passed, then we were taken by Lorries (British trucks) to a camp in Teheran. We were there several months and, again, taken to Ahvaz.

Gratitude: Reading through the material on Iran, I found that the Iranian people were most hospitable to us. The following also deserves our gratitude: Bishop Joseph Gawlina and the Sisters of Nazarethans who also were refugees. They primarily focused on helping the deserving orphans.

Our gratitude is also extended to the Carpathian Division Engineers; American, British, Hindu and Polish Soldiers who played a huge role in our survival!

We, refugees, did not stay in Iran long because:
1.Of the hostility of Soviet Authorities who occupied Northern Iran.
2.Threats from German Armies who were in close proximity to Iran (fighting in Caucuses located north of Iran).

In 1943 the British Government stopped recognizing the "Polish Government-in-Exile" in London. The power was given to the newly formed "Lubin Government" (Communists) in the Soviet occupied Poland. What this meant was that Poles could be repatriated back to Russia's Poland. We did not want to go back and live under Communism.

What to do with the Refugees that are Left?

Now what is to be done with all the refugees that were in Iran?

In 1942, the British Government made exhaustive efforts to find countries that would take us. America, Canada, and several South American countries were approached. They refused to take us at that time. Mexico was approached and they accepted. A large number were sent there. Our second cousins, Karolina Opalka and her remaining three children, Danuta, Stanislaw, and Edward were sent to Santa Rosa, Mexico from India. Karolina's husband and two sons all died in Uzbekistan—two from Typhus. What a heart-breaking story they have to tell. Stanislaw (Stanley) a history teacher (in the U.S.) wrote their story "Escape from Russia" which was published in 2004.

Great Britain decided to open up their territories to us. We, the women, children, older men, and orphans were resettled in the following countries:

Lebanon established two Camps:

1. Ajaltoun

2. Zouk Mikael

Palestine—2 Camps

1. Jerusalem

2. Ain Karem

India—2 Camps

1.Balachadi-Jamnagar

2.Valivade-Kolhapur

New Zealand—1 Camp

1. Pahiatua (for orphans)

Mexico–– 1 Camp

1.Santa Rosa

And the continent of Africa opened up her colonies to the majority of the people.

Uganda—2 Camps

1.Masindi

2.Kojo

Northern Rhodesia (Now Zambia) 4 Camps

1. Livingston

2.Lusaka

3.Bwana M'Kubwa

4.Abercorn

Southern Rhodesia (Now Zimbabwe)

1. Rusape

2. Diggleford

3. MARAHDELLAS

It is now (2015) a dictatorship under President Mugabe.

South Africa—1 Camp

1.Oudtshoorn

Kenya–1 Camp

1. Rongai

Tanganyika 4 Camps

1. Tengeru-we were in this camp.
2.Infunda
3.Kondoa
4.Morogoro

The Polish deportees (later renamed "Displaced Persons") were resettled throughout 23 camps that spanned 11 countries. Then in 1947 and 1948 when these camps were closed –we again had to find other countries that would accept us so that we could live out our lives.

Back to Iran:

While still in Ahvaz, Iran, Mom, Zofia and I traveled to Basra, Iraq with many others. Shortly we boarded a war ship there. We sailed on the Persian Gulf, Gulf of Oman, Arabian Sea, and Indian Ocean. A week passed and we docked at Mombasa a port in Kenya, Africa. We are unsure of the date of arrival there as we have no documents as proof. Our destination was to live in Camp Tengeru, Tanganyika for the next five years.

TANGANYIKA
AFRICA

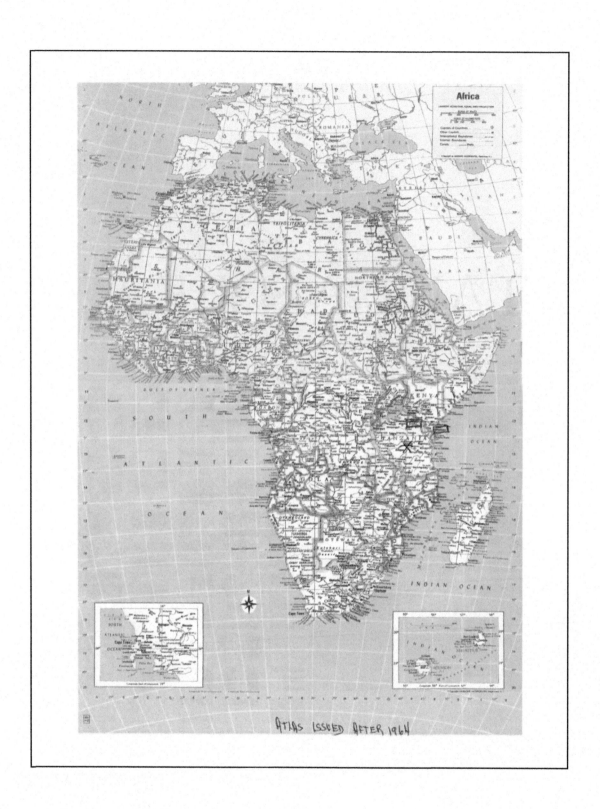

ATLAS ISSUED AFTER 1964

In 1964, Tanganyika merged with Zanzibar and was renamed Tanzania.
Mom, Zofia, and I were sent to Camp Tengeru, Tanganyika.
(Refer to Large Map-and follow the route from #4 Pahlavi, Iran to
#5 Tanganyika).

History: Tanganyika was a German Colony up to 1919. When Germany
lost W.W. 1, the country was taken over by The League of Nations
becoming a British Trust Territory. When the United Nations was created
in 1942, it continued to be a U.N. Trust Territory with Great Britain
managing it. Tanganyika's Capital was and presently is Dar-Es-Salaam, a
seaport on the Indian Ocean. Camp Tengeru was on the equator in North
Eastern Tanganyika.

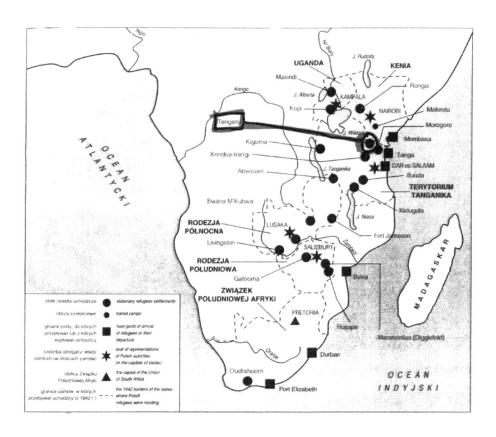

Before we arrived, the Negroes armed with axes and saws had to clear the overgrowth inside the camp and the jungle next to it. Because a big part of the jungle was cleared most of the large animals moved to the forest at the foot of Mount Meru.

The camp had a view of the highest peak in Africa which is Mount Kilimanjaro (See Photo).

harcerską, katolicką i polskiej YMCA. Co uderzało w tym osiedlu najbardziej, to egzotyczna przyroda oraz prymitywna, dalece niekompletna zabudowa i urządzenia sanitarne, a także brak wszelkiego sprzętu, co dawało się szczególnie odczuć w szpitalu i szkołach. I w tym wszystkim wysoki poziom organizacji osiedla, w którym życie toczyło się normalnie. Brakowało podręczników; elementarze były przepisywane; książki dla klas starszych zastępowano materiałem wybranym według naszego programu z przypadkowo zdobytych obcojęzycznych podręczników i książek popularnych. Funkcjonował sierociniec,

pracował pełną parą szpital osiedlowy. Życie harcerskie kwitło. Obejmowało większość dzieci i młodzieży jako jedyna organizacja, która potrafiła obywać się bez świetlic, sprzętu sportowego, bez bibliotek, nawet bez kwalifikowanych instruktorów. Pracowała dzięki pamięci pojedynczych osób dorosłych i garstki starszej młodzieży. Znano tekst przyrzeczenia harcerskiego i prawo harcerskie oraz wiele piosenek harcerskich. Poszyto mundury harcerskie przedwojennego kroju. Z osób, z którymi zetknęłam się w Tengeru, największe wrażenie zrobiła na mnie Eugenia Grosicka, kierująca dużym

sierocińcem, przy którym działał też mały dom starców. Jednocześnie była w osiedlu hufcowa. Hufiec harcerski w Tengeru był liczny, zwłaszcza jeśli chodzi o dziewczęta. Podzielony był na dwie zasadnicze części: drużyny harcerek i gromady zuchów dziewcząt oraz drużyny harcerzy i gromady zuchów chłopców; prowadzili je przyboczni hufcowej – Madzia Jarosz i Witek Kozak. Był to hufiec harcerski z prawdziwego zdarzenia. Urządzał obozy nawet w tym najwcześniejszym okresie, kiedy nie było jeszcze żadnego sprzętu, a co najważniejsze – namiotów. Radzono sobie stawiając namioty z koców,

Polskie osiedle uchodźcze Tengeru w okręgu Arusha położone było niewiele na południe od równika, z widokiem na ośnieżony stożek Kilimandżaro – różowy o zachodzie słońca, srebrzystoniebieski o wschodzie. Na ten najwyższy szczyt górski Afryki, prawie 6 tys. m wysokości, w czasie naszego pobytu w Afryce wyszły z Tengeru trzy wyprawy z udziałem Polaków. Byli to m.in.: hm. dr Wiktor Szyryński i dh. Stanisław Czernek, phm. Jan Barycz dh Mirosław Krążyński i S. Czernek (powtórnie), Jakub Hofmann i Maria Sidor, nauczyciele. Jako pierwszy z Polaków zdobył ten szczyt dr Antoni Jakubski w 1910 r.

The view of the Kilimanjaro Mt. from the Polish refug settlement Tengeru

from Book
EXILED CHILDREN

Another mountain, Meru, a dormant volcano was in close proximity to our camp (See Photo).

Moje Tengeru

Napisanie kilk   ...oćby zdań o pobycie grupy „wychodźców polskich" w Afryce Wschodniej nakazuje w moim przypadku powrót do Tengeru. Powrót? – Ale czy było rozstanie? – Więc nie! – Nie było. Bo najpierw musiałabym rozstać się zupełnie z pamięcią własną i ze swoją tożsamością nawet.

Osiedle nasze składało się z domków zbudowanych w „stylu afrykańskim". Ich stożkowate dachy kryte fartuchami z liści bananowych czy też trawy słoniowej były przeżuwane dniem i nocą przez niestrudzone termity. Dawało to charakterystyczne efekty dźwiękowe (niezbyt miłe zresztą). We

wnętrzu znajdowało się niewiele ...ętów: łóżka, stół, taborety i coś w rodzaju szafy – stelaż obity tkaniną kocową. Kuchnia, właściwie palenisko tylko, znajdowała się na otwartej przestrzeni, pod daszkiem dającym osłonę przed deszczem i upałem. Sanitariaty były wspólne. Ich standard też nie był wysokiej klasy.

Za to każdy prawie domek okolony był ogródkiem kwiatowym, w którym rosły nostalgiczne malwy, cynie, balsaminki czy róże, ale także i bardziej egzotyczne kanny, krzewy gwiazdy betlejemskiej i datury, odurzającej zapachem swych kwiatów, drzewa papai i nie znane mi z nazwy pnącza

Przy wjeździe do osiedla witał każdego napis „Polska" – po angielsku aby był zrozumiały dla tamtejszych ludzi.

There was a welcoming sign „Poland" at the

Previous eruptions from Mount Meru made the soil very fertile for farming. Also close by was beautiful Lake Duluti. Several miles from the camp were the town of Arusha which had a bus depot and a train station. The people living there were British, Indians and Arabs who had businesses. The natives worked for them. In close proximity to the camp were plantations of coffee, bananas and sugar cane owned by the affluent.

In charge of all camps in Africa were retired British Army officers. The administration and the daily management of each camp was left in the hands of the Poles.

When Mom and I docked in Mombasa, Kenya we were transported to Camp Tengeru, Tanganyika.

Note: Father's mother, Katarzyna, his sister, Karolina Opalka and her three daughters Krystyna, Helena, and Leonka were sent from Iran to Camp Masindi in Uganda. As of this writing June 2015, the only one that is still living is Krystyna in New Jersey with whom I am in contact.

Separation:

At this time, we were separated from:

1. Zofia who was held back in Iran because she was sick. She later traveled with a hospital unit and when she reached Tengeru she was directly taken to the Camp's Hospital.

2. Dad was in Iraq with the Army.

3. Janina was in Poland.

4. Zdzislaw and Antoni were either in India or already at Camp Makindu, Kenya.

Mom was assigned a hut in Group 5. Our houses were white-washed round huts. Roofs were thatched with banana or palm leaves. There was one room, one door, one window, no screens, and a packed down dirt floor. Inside we had four single beds, mattresses filled with sisal, an abundant native plant. Nets covered our beds to protect us from mosquitoes, especially the Anopheles which caused Malaria. There was a table and chairs in the center, also a shelf to hold clothes and utensils etc.

Once my brothers arrived a rope draped with a blanket provided privacy. A round basin was used to wash ourselves. A large one was available for bathing and was passed around from family to family. We had a kerosene lamp for light. Water was brought in daily from a well that had a faucet.

A separate rectangular mud building was a communal toilet facility. See picture of hut.

TANGANIKA

from Book: EXILED CHILDREN

Food supplies were satisfactory. We ate at a dining hall where meals were cooked. Women could use this facility to cook food themselves if it was not in use. One main road ran in front of our hut.

Conditions were primitive but finally we were free from oppression!! Yet, this "Black Land" frightened mothers as they were scared for their children. The women never wanted to be resettled in Africa—the very continent that offered them hospitality. But for the boys to live there, it was intriguing. Mothers' concerns regarding the natives soon vanished as she found them non-threatening and friendly. They clapped their hands in moments of joy, they hummed and sang while at work or play. The natives were from the Masai/Bantu Tribe and spoke Swahili. Men were half naked covered with a blanket tied over one shoulder. The women covered with colorful cloth adorned themselves with many necklaces and earrings.

There was a market and an orphanage near the camp's hospital. Here the natives sold chickens, eggs, but mostly fruit. You could buy three different kinds of bananas, juicy mangoes, succulent papayas, coconuts and later we discovered topi-topi (which is similar in looks to kiwi fruit but does not taste the same.) How wonderful it was to enjoy these new fruits!

Mom, Zofia, and I were settled in the camp. Mom found out through the International Red Cross that Janina was all right and still in her aunt's care in Poland. She thanked God that she was safe. Father also was in touch with us. He was a baker/cook in the army now in Palestine. To my knowledge no fighting took place in Palestine.

The first bad incident that happened in Tengeru involved me. I was around four. Our hut was next to a main road which had extraordinarily little traffic. I ran onto the road and was struck by a truck. My back near my right hip was bashed in and my right leg was broken. The impact caused enormous bruising. I was taken to the hospital. There was no anesthesia or strong pain killing medicine available. They did their absolute best to set my leg and take care of my hip area. When the leg was almost healed the doctor found my leg was crooked. He re-broke the bone and reset it. Mom said when that took place I screamed and begged her to suffocate me. Well, I lived and healed. The only reminder of that accident is a huge mark in back of my hip.

It took close to two years to locate Zdzislaw and Antoni through the Red Cross. My brothers finally arrived in Tengeru from Kenya. When Antoni came off the truck, he was skinny, but when Zdzislaw appeared everyone was shocked! He was so very thin that Mom and the neighbors thought he had T.B. What a heartbreak for Mom. To welcome the boys, she and Zofia baked Packzi (jelly buns). Both boys could not stop eating them.

Also, they were hiding some for later. Mom reassured them that they would never go hungry again and over time both boys recovered strength and gained weight. Once strong my brothers were a blessing to our family. The first thing they did was build a fireplace next to our hut. They would gather branches and weather permitting, Mom and Zofia would cook for us. Later on, the boys raised chickens (4 or 5) mainly for eggs. They built a chicken coop on a tree next to our hut and trained them to go up and down the ladder. This kept the chickens safe. How smart of them to do that. The boys also raised rabbits for food.

School:

There were 19,000 refugees that settled in African camps. Half of that number were school aged children and many more that would soon need it. All children had suffered a delay in learning and their normal development had been interrupted because of their experiences of the previous three years.

Great effort was made to make up for this deprivation. To obtain normalcy for them the task of building schools took place. The buildings were the same as our huts but rectangular. The inside lacked good lighting as no windows were installed. The only light and ventilation came in through openings from the roof-line extending downward around 3 to 4 feet on all four walls.

Another hurdle to overcome was the lack of teachers. The camps had a small percentage of educated women. Some were relocated from other camps. Many were brought in from Cyprus (Many Poles ended up in Cyprus. They traveled through Romania when the war broke out in Poland.) Cyprus belonged to Britain at that time. Zofia said that her classes were exceptionally large —well over 40 students. There were only a few textbooks. The students relied on their notes which were always incomplete. Zofia used to say: "If only Janina was with us. She would be a great help to me with my studies!"

Mom and Zofia missed Janina greatly. She was always on Mom's mind and she was always wondering how she was.

Once functioning, elementary classes were through the 6th grade. High School for general studies, business, fashion (pattern making and sewing,) agriculture and trade schools for mechanics were also formed. School hours were from 8:00 AM to 1:00 PM because of the afternoon heat. School was closed one month in the summer. In the winter, school was closed during the rainy season which was November through January; and, unfortunately, was also interrupted by the many outbreaks of Malaria.

I started my schooling in Tengeru. Zdzislaw and Antoni resumed

elementary classes (See Photo.)

ALTER BOYS at THE ENTRANCE of OUR CHURCH
w/ ANTONI

HELENA'S PRESCHOOL w/ FATHER SLIWOWSKI
1945-46

Zofia completed her elementary schooling. She continued high school in the field of commerce (business.) See Photo.

Zofia working in
Store 1946
17 yrs old

Helens
1st Communion
Sept 30, 1947

One of Zofia's classes

Church:

Father Dziduszko, our first priest, started the building of a church in the center of the camp. Soon Father Jan Sliwowski came. He completed building it. All flocked to church to thank God for sparing their lives, praying for family members in the army and elsewhere and for all those who never made it out of Russia. Our camp, the largest, had 4,000 women, their children, orphans, and some elderly men. Father Jan could have been overwhelmed by the large Catholic population for the majority of people were Catholic. Yet Father found time to teach several courses in school. The two priests issued birth certificate affidavits, started many religious organizations, had processions for holy days (See photo) and much more.

Polskie Osiedle, Tengeru. TANGANYIKA

1943 or 1944

ARUSHA - SMALL CITY BY CAMP TENGERU

Procession with Cardinal - Father Sliwowski

(Harcerki) Girl Scouts (Zofia)

After Father Jan left, his replacement was Father Piotr Roginski. His health was seriously damaged in Russia's labor camp. He still performed his duties faithfully. He loved his parishioners and especially the young people. He worked hard to occupy their leisure time and to keep the boys from mischief.

Our Neighbors: (See Photo below)
A family that lived next to us was Mrs. Jablonska who had two boys and a daughter. There was Mrs. Opalka (no relation to us) who had two boys, Gienek and Witek and a daughter.

Antoni, Zofia, Helena, Mom Katarzyna & Zdzistaw Rodzinka Camp Tengeru, Tanganyika, Africa (1946) in front of our hut

Some of our neighbors - GROUP 5 Camp Tengeru

A tragedy befell a lady that lived in back of our hut. She had one son. He went swimming with a group of boys in a nearby river. This boy jumped into the water from a dock. He came up rapidly under the dock and hit his head into some protruding nails. He died. Our whole group was deeply saddened by this tragedy.

In this tropical climate the youngsters developed rapidly. Suddenly most of the boys and girls who arrived frail developed into young men and women. But as the boys grew older so did problems. There were few jobs for them to do because no one could work outside the camp. The situation that made it worse was the fact that every home was fatherless.

Besides chores around our hut my brothers had one job in the camp. It was during the one month of summer vacation. They were to keep intact the reclaimed camp from the jungle. They cut down bushes, shrubs and cleared vegetation from irrigation ditches at the only vegetable garden belonging to the camp. Mom worked in that garden. Peanuts, sweet potatoes, and tomatoes were grown.

With plenty of leisure time the places where the boys could disappear in were many. The first place for the boys to disappear in was the jungle which was in back of our Group 5 huts. It was full of hanging vines, monkeys, and snakes. A few times I followed my brothers to the outskirts of the jungle, they yelled and told me to go back home, that I was too young to follow them plus girls were not welcome.

A second hiding place for the boys was the lake and the overgrowth of the river. A third hiding place was the Masai Market Place and the native village. And fourth our camp was sprawled over a large area in all directions. While in the borders of the camp the boys were still far from home. Once Zdzislaw did his chores he left with his friends and was gone until dark. Remember school was out by 1PM. He allowed Antoni to go with him once in a while. Zdzislaw told me that he did not study. Late in the evening Zofia had to help him with his homework. Mom disciplined the boys…she did not spare the rod. In spite of their mischievous ways, both boys grew up to be hard working, responsible men. Yet the boy's disobedience to stay close to their homes produced two benefits:

1. Spending time with the natives in their village and market the boys quickly learned Swahili which was a great advantage for our family and the families of the other boys.

2. The boy's exploration of the jungle and the lake shore advanced their exposure to a variety of monkeys, snakes, and birds such as the Toucans, Sun Birds (similar to our hummingbirds,) Birds of Paradise and Ostrich. Occasionally, we would get to eat an ostrich egg. They were huge and would feed several of us.

Opposite to the boy's adventurous ways, the girls stayed inside the camp borders (organized tours were O.K.) and were a big help to their mothers. This was true of Zofia. She studied hard, helped take care of me when Mom worked. She and Mom mended clothing and sewed dresses. Zofia embroidered cloths to cover the table, cross stitched beautiful patterns on burlap that became decorative pillows or wall hangings for our hut, a hut with no basic conveniences and with a dirt floor! I still have some of her beautiful work to this day. Zofia did go with her friends to the civic center, to see movies and to attend scouting meetings; but she had no problems missing some activities for she knew she was needed at home and that was her priority.

ANTONI - white
        Swatki
  x Idsistaw

Najważniejsze w polskich osiedlach uchodźczych były
szkoły. Na zdjęciu trzecia klasa męskiej szkoły
powszechnej z wychowawczynią Anna Tyrkowa

Third class of the elementary school for boys with their
class teacher, Anna Tyrkowa

from Book:
TUŁACZE - DZIECI
      or
  EXILED CHILDREN

x Zdzisław

Ta sama klasa, z ta sama wychowawczynią w trzy lata
później, tak ci chłopcy wydorośleli, kiedy już kończą
szkołę powszechną

The same class and the same teacher three years later

Zofia

_W Tengeru było kilka szkół średnich. Oto uczennice
klasy I b Gimnazjum Kupieckiego z wychowawczynią,
Jadwigą Batycka_

{ _Class 1b of the Commercial Gymnasium with their class
teacher, Jadwiga Batycka_ }

from Book
TUŁACZE
DZIECI
or
EXILED CHILDREN

_Średnia Szkoła Rolnicza: lekcja botaniki przy
mikroskopie, dla lepszego oświetlenia pod gołym
niebem. Stoi nauczyciel biologii, inż. Henryk
Brzostowski; przy mikroskopie (w ciemnej sukience)
Jadzia Śmietana_

_Secondary School of Agriculture: a botany lesson with
a microscope, conducted outdoors for better
lighting_

For the mothers with many children things were difficult. They labored washing clothes, cooking (the community kitchen closed after a certain time.) Mom also worked in the camp's garden. It was back breaking work in the merciless heat of the tropics. She was an incredible Mom! Take a look at our photos in Tengeru! Observe how clean, well pressed and dressed we all were for church and school. You can see how impeccable the Girl Scout uniforms were, the garb for the altar boys—how wonderful everyone looked. I cannot comprehend how this was possible. Living in a small, one room hut, no indoor toilets, bathtub, no laundry conveniences and yet we looked as though we could have been standing in front of an American house that had all those conveniences!

Health problems plagued us. Fleas called Jigras were parasites that lodged themselves primarily under the toenails. This was a pervasive problem as sandals were mainly worn. Red ants, soldier ants and termites were destructive there. But the worst problem was Malaria. The symptoms were high fever, shivering, aching bones, and violent headaches; and Malaria spared almost no one. Even after treatment with Atabrin and Quinine the sickness came back again and again. Everyone in my family had Malaria, but Zdzislaw's reoccurring bouts brought him close to death. The concern was so great that the English "Mayor" and his wife visited our hut.

The Church was the heart:
For us, the Church was the heart of our family life. Mom was very devout. We always attended Mass on Sunday and Holy Days. We were involved in church functions and organizations. In the five to six years the Polish refugees spent in Tengeru, the adults took on hard responsibilities and made the education, organizations, Polish culture, and customs thrive. Leaning on our God and Savior, Jesus Christ, the inhabitants went from meagerness to building a thriving community life for the people.

With the end of WWII, the Polish Army was transported to England for discharge. Those women and children who had fathers or brothers in the Army were the first to leave these camps and sail for England as all camps were scheduled to close by 1947. Because of difficult circumstances the time for closing was prolonged.

For the second time organizations had to find countries that would accept families who no longer had anyone in the army. Those families as well as orphans were not entitled to go to England. Therefore, these families were eventually sent to Australia, Argentina, Brazil, Venezuela, Mexico, and Canada. Orphans in African camps were sent to New Zealand, Canada as well as Italy.

Because Dad was in the Army, we were one of the first families to be issued
"Temporary Certificates" to travel to the United Kingdom.
(See Certificates.)

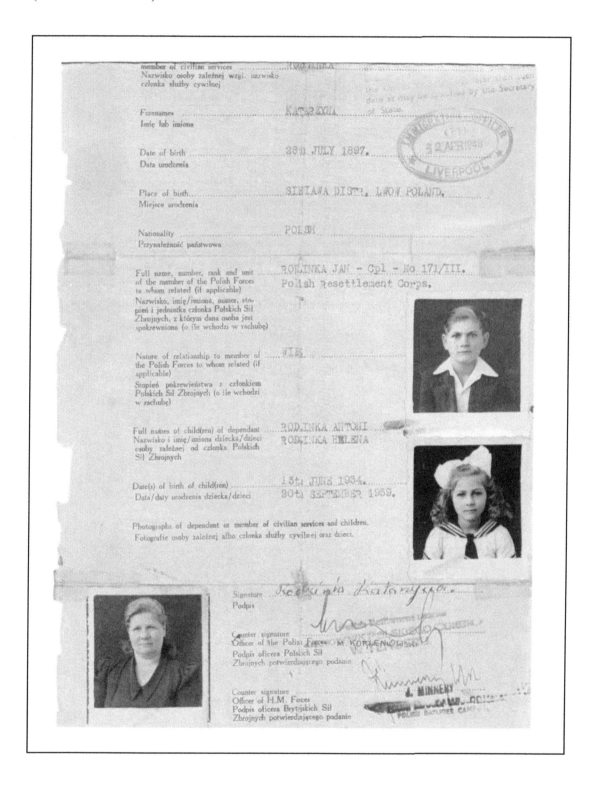

Temporary Certificate to be held by dependants of members of the Polish Forces or by members of civilian services attached to the Polish Forces, entering the United Kingdom.

Tymczasowe Zaswiadczenie dla osob zależnych od członkow Polskich Sil Zbrojnych przybywających do Zjednoczonego Krolestwa, jak rowniez dla członkow sluzby cywilnej zwiazanej z Polskimi Silami Zbrojnymi, ktorzy przybywaja rowniez do Zjednoczonego Krolestwa.

The present temporary certificate is issued in order to provide dependants of members of the Polish Forces or members of civilian services attached to the Polish Forces with a document of identity to enable them to enter the United Kingdom. It is without prejudice to and in no way affects the national status of the holder. The temporary certificate remains valid so long as the holder remains in the United Kingdom and does not obtain a national passport. If the holder wishes to go abroad, application should be made for a fresh Certificate of Identity to —

H.M. Chief Inspector,
Immigration Branch,
Home Office,
10, Old Bailey,
London, E.C.4.

2 6 JAN 1951

All persons of 16 and over require a separate certificate, but the particulars relating to children under 16 may be entered on a parent's certificate.

Celem niniejszego tymczasowego zaswiadczeni jest zaopatrzenie osob zależnych od członków Polskich Sil Zbrojnych oraz członków sluzby cywilnej zwiazanej z Polskimi Silami Zbrojnymi dokumentem tożsamości, na podstawie którego będą one wpuszczone do Zjednoczonego Królestwa. To tymczasowe zaswiadczenie, które ani nie przesądza ani nie ma wplywu na sprawę przynależności państwowej właściciela, będzie ważne na czas pobytu właściciela w Zjednoczonym Królestwie, o ile nie otrzyma on normalnego paszportu.

4322.T.

Permitted to land on condition that the Holder...

Surname of the dependant or

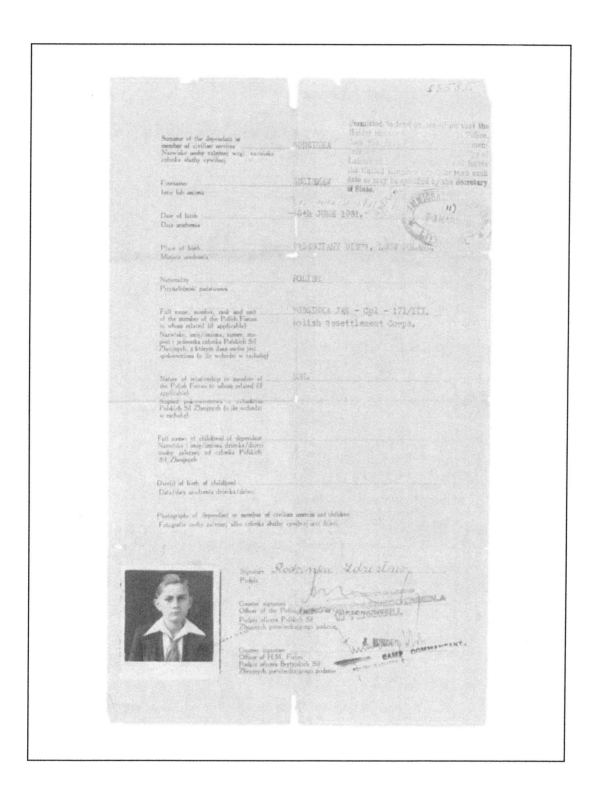

Surname of the dependant or
member of civilian services
Nazwisko osoby zależnej wzgl. nazwisko
członka służby cywilnej _____ RODZINKA

Forenames
Imię lub imiona _____ BOLESŁAW

Permitted to land on condition that the
Holder _____ Police,
and _____ ent
Land_____ ty of
the United Kingdom _____ than such
date as may be specified by the Secretary
of State.

Date of birth
Data urodzenia _____ 5th JUNE 1931.

Place of birth
Miejsce urodzenia _____ PRZEMYANY MIRTM, LŁOW POLAND.

Nationality
Przynależność państwowa _____ POLISH

Full name, number, rank and unit
of the member of the Polish Forces
to whom related (if applicable)
Nazwisko, imię/imiona, numer, stopień i jednostka członka Polskich Sił
Zbrojnych, z którym dana osoba jest
spokrewniona (o ile wchodzi w rachubę) _____ RODZINKA JAN - Cpl - 171/III.
Polish Resettlement Corps.

Nature of relationship to member of
the Polish Forces to whom related (if
applicable)
Stopień pokrewieństwa w członkiem
Polskich Sił Zbrojnych (o ile wchodzi
w rachubę) _____ SON.

Full name of children of dependant
Nazwisko i imię/imiona dziecka/dzieci
osoby zależnej od członka Polskich
Sił Zbrojnych

Date(s) of birth of children
Data/daty urodzenia dziecka/dzieci

Photographs of dependant or member of civilian services and children
Fotografie osoby zależnej albo członka służby cywilnej oraz dzieci

Signature
Podpis _____ *Rodzinka Zdzisław*

Counter signature
Officer of the Polish Forces _____
Podpis oficera Polskich Sił
Zbrojnych potwierdzającego podanie

Counter signature
Officer of H.M. Forces
Podpis oficera Brytyjskich Sił
Zbrojnych potwierdzającego podanie _____ CAMP COMMANDANT.

Form 223X.

Temporary Certificate to be held by dependants of members of the Polish Forces or by
members of civilian services attached to the Polish Forces, entering the United Kingdom.

Tymczasowe Zaświadczenie dla osób zależnych od członków Polskich Sił Zbrojnych
przybywających do Zjednoczonego Królest a, jak również dla członków służby cywilnej
związanej z Polskimi Siłami Zbrojnymi, I órzy przybywają również do Zjednoczonego
Królestwa.

The present temporary certificate is issued in order to provide dependants of members of the Polish
Forces or members of civilian services attached to the Polish Forces with a document of identity to
enable them to enter the United Kingdom. It is without prejudice to and in no way affects the national status
of the holder. The temporary certificate remains valid so long as the holder remains in the United
Kingdom and does not obtain a national passport. If the holder wishes to go abroad, application
should be made for a fresh Certificate of Identity to :—

H.M. Chief Inspector,
Immigration Branch,
Home Office,
10, Old Bailey,
London, E.C.4.

All persons of 16 and over require a separate certificate, but the particulars relating to children
under 16 may be entered on a parent's certificate.

Celem niniejszego tymczasowego zaświadczenia jest zaopatrzenie osób zależnych od członków Polskich
Sił Zbrojnych oraz członków służby cywilnej związanej z Polskimi Siłami Zbrojnymi dokumentem tożsamości, na podstawie którego będą one wpuszczone do Zjednoczonego Królestwa. To tymczasowe zaświadczenie, które ani nie przesądza ani nie ma wpływu na sprawę przynależności państwowej właściciela, będzie
ważne na czas pobytu właściciela w Zjednoczonym Królestwie, o ile nie otrzyma on normalnego paszportu.
Właściciel tymczasowego zaświadczenia, który chce wyjechać zagranicę, powinien skierować podanie o nowe
zaświadczenie tożsamości pod następującym adresem:

H.M. Chief Inspector,   Naczelny Dyrektor,
Immigration Branch,   Wydział Imigracyjny,
Home Office,   Ministerstwo Spraw Wewnętrznych,
10, Old Bailey,   10, Old Bailey,
London. E.C.4.   London. E.C.4.

Osoby które ukończyły szesnaście (16) lat, powinne posiadać osobne zaświadczenia, dane zaś dotyczące
dzieci poniżej szesnastu (16) lat mogą być wpisane do zaświadczenia ojca wzgl. matki.

Our family of 5 left Camp Tengeru by train traveling north to Mombasa, Kenya. At Mombasa, we boarded the ship ORBITA.

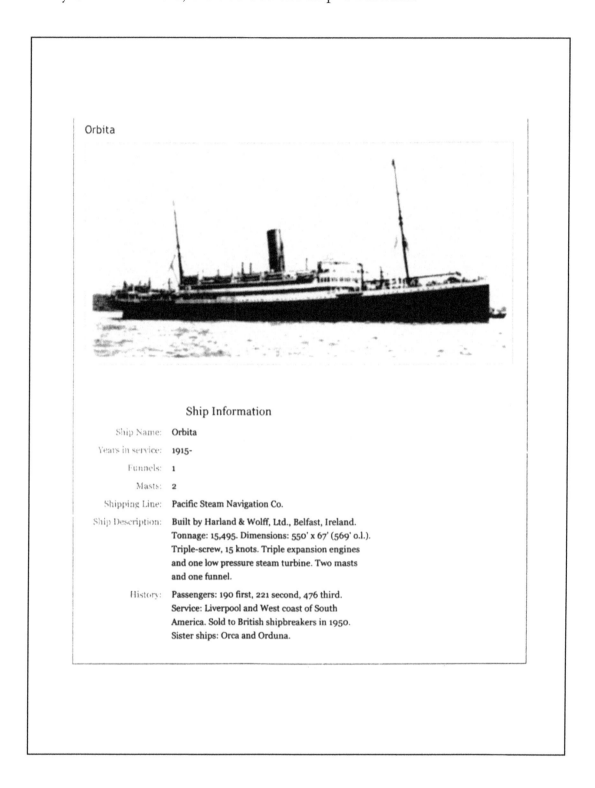

Orbita

Ship Information

Ship Name:	**Orbita**
Years in service:	**1915-**
Funnels:	**1**
Masts:	**2**
Shipping Line:	**Pacific Steam Navigation Co.**
Ship Description:	**Built by Harland & Wolff, Ltd., Belfast, Ireland. Tonnage: 15,495. Dimensions: 550' x 67' (569' o.l.). Triple-screw, 15 knots. Triple expansion engines and one low pressure steam turbine. Two masts and one funnel.**
History:	**Passengers: 190 first, 221 second, 476 third. Service: Liverpool and West coast of South America. Sold to British shipbreakers in 1950. Sister ships: Orca and Orduna.**

See the picture of ORBITA ship's log and picture of the U.K. Passenger Log.

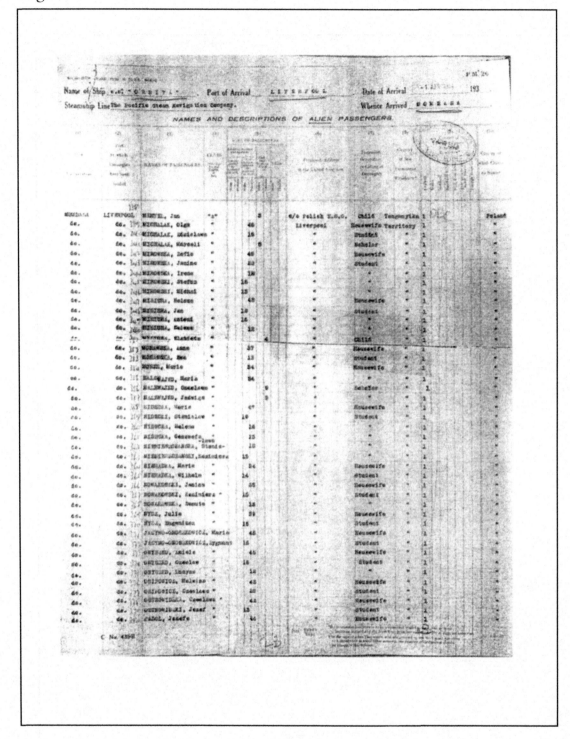

Note: Zdzislaw's name is missing from the ship's log and passenger log sailing north on the Red Sea through the Suez Canal we docked at Port Said in Egypt. We saw many people on the docks shouting and waving to us. While there, without any explanation, about fifteen youths were taken off our ship and transferred onto another. Zdzislaw and Antoni were among them.

UK Incoming Passenger Lists, 1878–1960

Name:	**Helena Rodzinka**
Birth Date:	**abt 1940**
Age:	**8**
Port of Departure:	**Mombasa, Kenya**
Arrival Date:	**1 Apr 1948**
Port of Arrival:	**Liverpool, England**
Ports of Voyage:	**Mombasa, Aden, Port Said and Larnaca**
Ship Name:	Orbita
Search Ship Database:	View the 'Orbita' in the 'Passenger Ships and Images' database
Shipping Line:	**The Pacific Steam Navigation Company**
Official Number:	**137467**

Source Citation: Class: *BT26*; Piece: *1233*; Item: *99*

Source Information:
Ancestry.com. *UK Incoming Passenger Lists, 1878-1960* [database on-line]. Provo, UT, USA: The Generations Network, Inc., 2008. Original data: *Board of Trade: Commercial and Statistical Department and successors: Inwards Passenger Lists*. Kew, Surrey, England: The National Archives of the UK (TNA). Series BT26, 1,472 pieces.
Data imaged from the National Archives, London, England. The National Archives gives no warranty as to the accuracy, completeness or fitness for the purpose of the information provided. Images may be used only for purposes of research, private study or education. Applications for any other use should be made to the National Archives, Kew, Richmond, Surrey TW9 4DU. Infringement of the above condition may result in legal action.

Description:
This database is an index to the Board of Trade's passenger lists of ships arriving in the United Kingdom from foreign ports outside of Europe and the Mediterranean from 1878-1888 and 1890-1960. Information listed on the passenger lists may include: name of passenger, their birth date or age, port of departure, port of arrival, date of arrival, and vessel name. **Learn more...**

UK Incoming Passenger Lists, 1878-1960

Name:	**Katarzyne Rodzinka**
Birth Date:	abt 1898
Age:	50
Port of Departure:	Mombasa, Kenya
Arrival Date:	1 Apr 1948
Port of Arrival:	Liverpool, England
Ports of Voyage:	Mombasa, Aden, Port Said and Larnaca
Ship Name:	Orbita
Search Ship Database:	View the 'Orbita' in the 'Passenger Ships and Images' database
Shipping Line:	The Pacific Steam Navigation Company
Official Number:	137467

Source Citation: Class: *BT26*; Piece: *1233*; Item: *99*

Source Information:
Ancestry.com. *UK Incoming Passenger Lists, 1878-1960* [database on-line]. Provo, UT, USA: The Generations Network, Inc., 2008. Original data: *Board of Trade: Commercial and Statistical Department and successors: Inwards Passenger Lists.* Kew, Surrey, England: The National Archives of the UK (TNA). Series BT26, 1,472 pieces.
Data imaged from the National Archives, London, England. The National Archives gives no warranty as to the accuracy, completeness or fitness for the purpose of the information provided. Images may be used only for purposes of research, private study or education. Applications for any other use should be made to the National Archives, Kew, Richmond, Surrey TW9 4DU. Infringement of the above condition may result in legal action.

Description:
This database is an index to the Board of Trade's passenger lists of ships arriving in the United Kingdom from foreign ports outside of Europe and the Mediterranean from 1878-1888 and 1890-1960. Information listed on the passenger lists may include: name of passenger, their birth date or age, port of departure, port of arrival, date of arrival, and vessel name. Learn more...

Once again, our family was separated! Mom was heart- broken as she did not know if she would see her sons again. Our ship left Port Said sailing on the Mediterranean Sea and reached the Island of Cyprus. There, new passengers boarded the Orbita. We now understand why the 15 or so boys had been removed from the ship at Port said so room would be made for these new passengers!

We continued on our voyage to England. Mom, Zofia, and I arrived in Liverpool, England on April 3, 1948.

(Refer to Large Map #1 from #5 to #6).

To our delight my brothers arrived safely before us. At this time all of us wanted to see Dad whom we had not seen for over 5 years.

Without a doubt, I know, Mom's joy was dampened as her heart and mind was on Stasiu who died in Uzbekistan and Janina who was left behind in Poland since the end of 1939! They were her first and second child that she gave birth to!

Next, we will tell the story of Poland's Armed Forces and Father's Service in Anders Army.

Note of Interest:
Uncle Felix Opalka, when in England, deposited all information regarding his service in the Anders Army with the SIKORSKY MUSEUM in London. This museum was in its infant stage of development. He named my brother, Antoni as his son and recorded this in official documents. How good of our Uncle to include Antoni in his family and call him his son!

POLAND'S ARMED FORCES

Including

Anders Army

Iran, Iraq, Palestine, Egypt, and Italy

See map and pictures of the service:

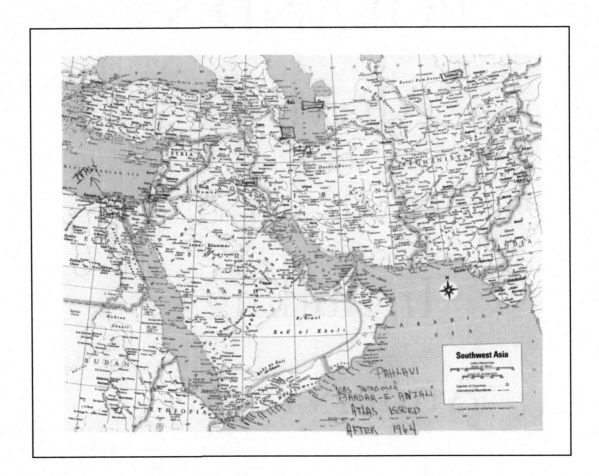

Poland's Armed Forces:

Poland was invaded by Germany and Russia in 1939, the following is a breakdown of our country's armed forces that fought protecting our land but also fought beyond our borders with the allies against enemy countries.

1. The established Armed Forces in Poland fought the two invading countries. They fought valiantly but the strength and numbers of the enemy was totally against them. Therefore, many were killed, sent to German Concentration Camps, deported to Soviet prisons with many of them killed or who died along the way. Those who survived fighting the hopeless battles in Poland joined the underground movement.

2. The Underground or "AK" (Armia Krajowa or Home Army) came into existence. The "Polish Jewish" resistance movement also sprang up. Although separate, both caused great damage to the Nazi military. The Home Army provided "Intelligence Services" sending it to London.

Note: Poles saved thousands of Jewish lives despite the fact that the penalty, if caught, was death.

3. When Poland was invaded by Germany many of Poland's Army, Navy, and Air Force fled to France. These branches reorganized under Great Britain and continued to fight the Nazis. They had the distinction of being the only nation to fight on every front in the war i.e., in France, in the Norwegian Campaign, at NARVIC. In Africa, the Carpathian Brigade fought at TOBRUK, squadrons fought at the Battle of Britain, took part in the D-Day landing, fought with Allies in the invasion of Europe, the liberation of France and other battles.

4. Polish Corps-Anders Army

(Refer to Large Map-follow route from #4 Iran to #4A Iraq, to #4B – Palestine to #-4C Egypt to #4D Italy)

Please read the attached article "Creation of the II Polish Corps."

Creation of the II Polish Corps

The II Polish Corps, under the command of Lt.General Wladyslaw Anders, was formed as a result of the Sikorski Maisky Agreement signed on December 4, 1941. After Germany's invasion of Russia, in June 1941, Stalin and Sikorski pledged mutual military support in the fight against a common enemy.

Part of the agreement dealt with the formation of a Polish army on Soviet soil, to fight alongside the Red Army against the Nazi threat. General Sikorski and General Anders met with Stalin to discuss the details of the Polish armament, conditional upon the release of all Polish prisoners held in Soviet camps.

When the Soviets invaded Poland in September 1939, the NKVD arrested and deported over 1.5 million Poles to Russian gulag where hundreds upon thousands of Poles suffered the most brutal of Soviet torture. Suddenly, Stalin agreed to the release of the Poles, granting them "amnesty" - their only "crime" was their resistance to Russian supremacy. Though Stalin led the Allies to believe that he would release them all, only a small number was given official permission to leave. Approximately 100,000 Poles were released from the camps. All efforts by Sikorski and Anders to obtain the release of the remaining prisoners failed.

Thousands of Polish military poured out of Soviet concentration camps, followed by thousands of civilians, men, women and children. Severely emaciated, starving and suffering from disease, many died trying to reach army checkpoints. Anders was anticipating the arrival of some 15,000 Polish officers, but none ever reported for duty. After an extensive inquiry and search, no trace of them could be found. Anders approached Stalin on numerous occasions demanding to know their whereabouts but was always met with evasion and lies. (Katyn) To make matters worse, the infamous NKVD, (the predecessor to todays KGB) took extraordinary measures to ensure that as many Poles as possible would perish. There were numerous instances where Polish refugees were forced to disembark from trains and convoys, and left stranded on the Russian steppes without supplies, food or water, while their transports went on without them.

Taking advantage of the terms of the Polish-Soviet Agreement, Stalin insisted on sending Polish army units to the front without providing them with reinforcements. Anders refused to permit this, calling it a wholesale slaughter of his men. Undeterred, Stalin reduced the food rations to the refugees from 70,000 to 26,000 soldiers. It was not enough to sustain them - there were over 115,000 Polish refugees, both military and civilian. In August 1942, Anders met with Churchill to discuss the organization of the Polish armed forces and plans to have them evacuated from Russia. It was agreed that they would be transferred to Persia (Iran) to serve under the command of General Wilson. This breakthrough gave Anders hope that Great Britain would not abandon Poland. After interminable postponements, Stalin finally agreed to an evacuation of the Polish refugees. News of the evacuation erupted in a violent flood of thousands upon thousands more Polish POWs heading towards Russian borders. Not all made it out in time. The remainder were trapped in Russia, not given official permission to leave.

The Polish army was also stationed in Iraq, camped out in tents under the blistering heat. Many men, women and children suffered bouts of malaria, but to the Poles it was nothing. They had already suffered worse. Training sessions took place all throughout the Middle East, but none so inspiring as that located in Gaza, Mount Sinai, and Nazareth - the Holy Land. In a short time, the men were miraculously transformed into healthy, strong fighting soldiers.

The 3rd Carpathian Rifle Division arrived in Palestine. They were formed from the Carpathian Infantry Brigade, under the command of Brigadier-General Stanislaw Kopanski, and under whose command fought brilliantly at Tobruk. Other troops which arrived were the Carpathian Lancers, the 12th Podbole Lancers, and the 15th Poznan Lancers, among many other Divisions. Just when the Polish forces were assembled and in excellent form,

Churchill approached Anders and obliged him to give up 3,500 of his best soldiers to reinforce the Polish Air Force in Great Britain. (They were to become a vital part of winning the Battle of Britain. See Kosciuszko Squadron) Anders complied.

During this time the Allies had landed on the Italian mainland - September 1943. Anders was again under intense

pressure from British Command to transfer several thousand more Polish troops to England. Anders strongly opposed this measure and argued that his army had to remain as strong as possible and to engage in battle as soon as possible. Meanwhile, the Soviet government had already set up the Union of Polish Patriots (UPP), a move which accelerated the already deteriorating relationship between Russia and Poland. The UPP forced the enlistment of vast number of Poles who had been prevented from leaving Russia during the evacuation.

By 1943, the II Polish Corps was fit, fully trained, and ready to engage in battle. In a letter to Anders on July 22, 1943, General Wilson expressed anticipation for the arrival of the Polish soldiers in Italy.

Within the rank and file of many Polish divisions and regiments, were also Polish-Jews, eager to serve their country. They were among the refugees released from the Russian gulag, and survived the long voyage to freedom with their Polish compatriots. Unfortunately, once the II Polish Corps landed in Palestine, a large contingent of Polish-Jewish servicemen deserted their posts. This came as a terrible blow to the Polish army virtually on the eve of battle and no doubt ignited not a little hostility towards the Jews. Nevertheless General Anders chose to grant them all amnesty. Despite this devastating setback, many Polish Jews remained committed

to fighting for Poland and remained in the army. They fought many battles including the Battle of Monte Cassino. Among the thousands of Poles killed in action there were many Polish Jews. Their tombstones, engraved with the

Star of David, can be found at Polish war cemeteries throughout Europe, and at Monte Cassino.

Besides the II Polish Corps, there were other Polish Divisions. During the _____ of 1939, the Polish army had evacuated Poland reorganizing its troops on French soil. There were only four divisions among the 85,000 troops - the First Grenadier Division, Second Infantry Fusiliers Division, 3rd and 4th Infantry Division - the 10th Brigade of Armored Cavalry, and 10ieme Brigade de cavalerie blindee making up the motorized Brigade, and the Polish Independent Highland Brigade, the latter having taken part in the 1940 Battle of Narvik.

After the fall of France, Sikorski evacuated many of the Polish troops to England, however only 25,000 of them were able to escape. In England, the I Polish Corps was formed, comprising of the Polish 1st Armored Division, the Polish Independent Parachute Brigade, and numerous other regiments. They trained in Scotland, defended the shores of Great Britain, fought the Battle of Normandy, the Battle of the Falaise Gap, and liberated many towns and villages in Belgium and Holland.

Creation of the Second Polish Corps - Polish Greatness

My Father joined the Anders Army as well as Felix Opalka, Dad's brother-in-law who was married to Dad's sister Karolina.

We have extraordinarily little information on Father's army life. You may recall that we parted with him in Iran. Mom, Zofia and I left Iran and sailed to Kenya. We then traveled to Camp Tengeru, Tanganyika.

From Iran, Father traveled with the Army to Iraq. They were there to convalesce from sicknesses as well as to build up everyone's strength from their weakened condition of the past 2 ½ years. From Iraq the army moved to Palestine. Training sessions took place throughout the Middle East. As the attached article points out the men were transformed into healthy and strong fighting soldiers.

Since Dad always was a good cook he enrolled and graduated from "KUHARSKIEJ SZKOLY" or Cooking School and that was what he did in the army. This job spared him from front–line battles.

(See picture of Cooking School Certificate).

PALESTINE 1943 - 1944
or EGYPT   City of GEDSRA?

Whatever location Dad was stationed in when in Palestine he the opportunity had to tour Jerusalem. I have many postcards of the Holy Land that are of most significance to us Christians.

The Route of the Polish Army:

I also have a "Jerusalem Cross" which is unique. From Palestine the Anders Army went to Egypt and then to Italy where they fought many battles. One of the most significant took place at Monte Cassino, town of Lazzio. A Benedictine Monastery stood on top. Many allied forces failed to defeat the Germans lodged on top of the mountain. When victory seemed unattainable the Anders Army defeated the Germans in May, 1944 but at an enormous price in lives. (See pictures of Monte Cassino next.)

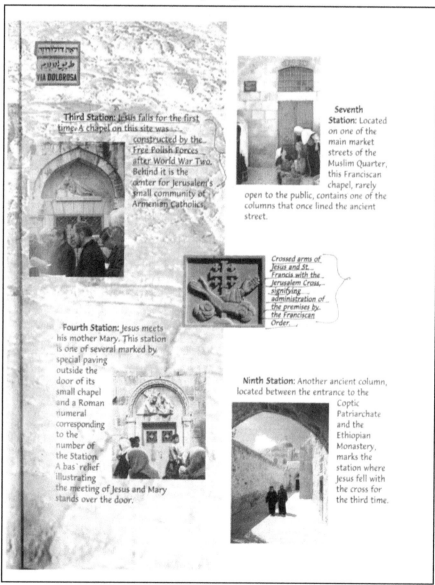

VIA DOLOROSA

Third Station: Jesus falls for the first time. A chapel on this site was constructed by the Free Polish Forces after World War Two. Behind it is the center for Jerusalem's small community of Armenian Catholics.

Seventh Station: Located on one of the main market streets of the Muslim Quarter, this Franciscan chapel, rarely open to the public, contains one of the columns that once lined the ancient street.

Crossed arms of Jesus and St. Francis with the Jerusalem Cross, signifying administration of the premises by the Franciscan Order.

Fourth Station: Jesus meets his mother Mary. This station is one of several marked by special paving outside the door of its small chapel and a Roman numeral corresponding to the number of the Station. A bas relief illustrating the meeting of Jesus and Mary stands over the door.

Ninth Station: Another ancient column, located between the entrance to the Coptic Patriarchate and the Ethiopian Monastery, marks the station where Jesus fell with the cross for the third time.

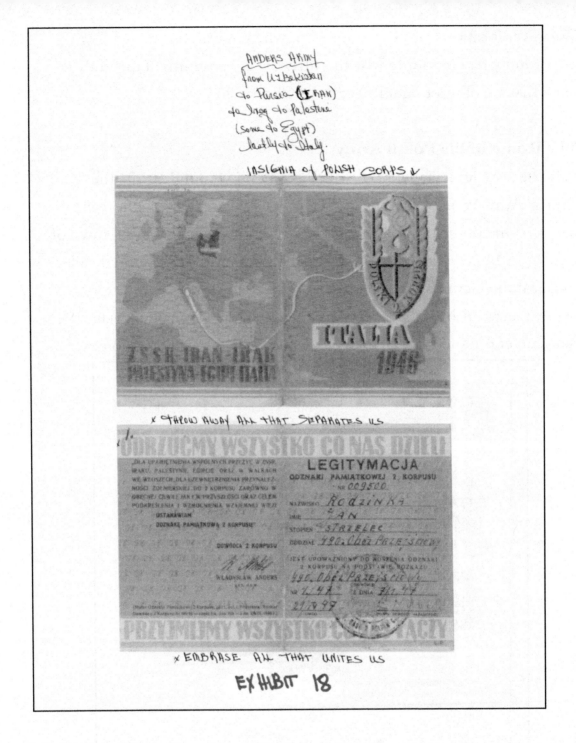

Harold MacMillan referred to General Ander's Army as one of the greatest fighting units in World War II winning battle after battle against Germany's finest soldiers. They opened up the road to Rome for the Allies.

(See The Insignia of the Polish Corps.)

BATTLE at MONTE CASSINO ITALY 1943–1945

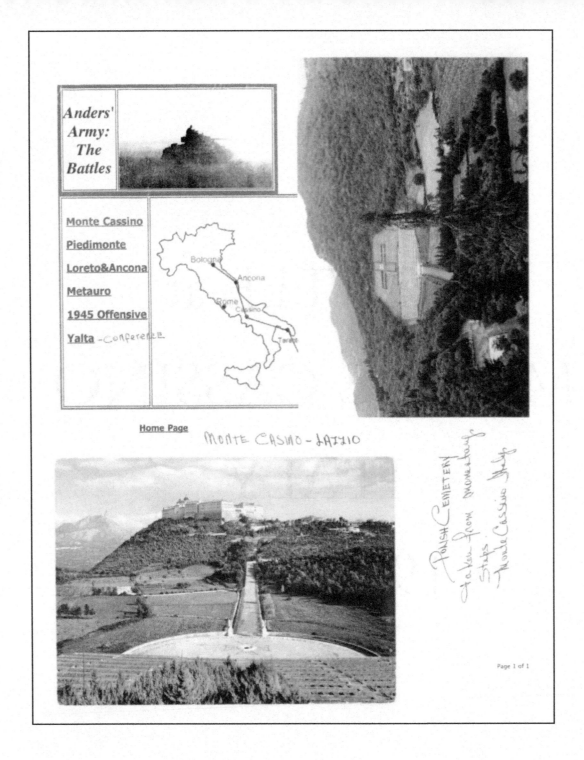

Anders'
Army:
The
Battles

Monte Cassino
Piedimonte
Loreto&Ancona
Metauro
1945 Offensive
Yalta - Conference

Bologna
Ancona
Rome
Cassino
Taranto

Home Page

MONTE CASINO - LAZIO

POLISH CEMETERY
taken from monastery
steps.
Monte Cassino Italy

Page 1 of 1

Tactical Air Force, against the German road and rail communications. By the end of March, twenty-five cuts on an average were made daily, and by mid-May they rose to seventy-five and even more. There can be no doubt that this sustained attack on the enemy's supply system, which not only interrupted his traffic but restricted him to night movements, did him far more damage than had any of the saturation bombing.

The Second Battle of the Garigliano was mounted and launched on May 11. This time Cassino itself was left alone.

The battle was opened by a night artillery bombardment of forty minutes of extreme intensity on a front of from thirty to forty miles. This time the infantry assault succeeded, partly on account of the air preparation and partly because the German winter line had now served its purpose; and, no longer supported by his ally, bad weather, Kesselring saw that the time to withdraw had come. On the night of May 16 he began to disengage his army; on the 17th, Cassino, turned from the rear, passed into British hands; and on the 18th, Monastery Hill was occupied by the Poles. On June 4 the Allied forces entered Rome, and two days later the news was flashed around the world that France had been invaded by the Americans and the British—a strategic second front had been opened.

Struggle for Italy: September 3, 1943. Successful Allied landings were made at Reggio Calabria, Taranto and Salerno. Stiff resistance by German defenders together with the rugged terrain combined to slow up the Allied advance. The fighting lasted twenty months.

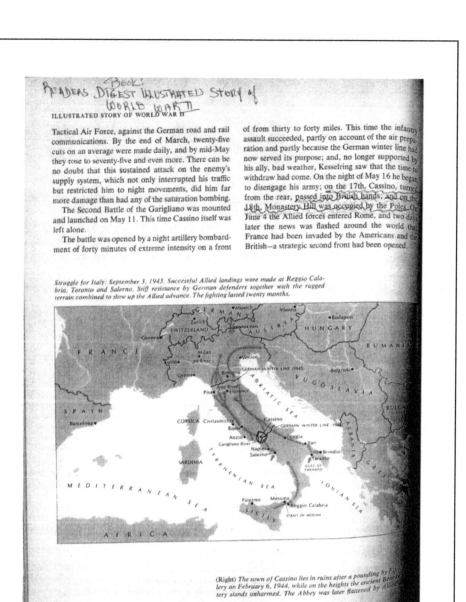

(Right) The town of Cassino lies in ruins after a pounding by Fifth artillery on February 6, 1944, while on the heights the ancient Benedictine Monastery stands unharmed. The Abbey was later flattened by Allied

340

During the battle they lost communication. These soldiers are trying to restore the radio link at Monte Cassino.

Monte Cassino tank

1.5 THOUSAND POLISH SOLDIERS
DIED AT MONTE CASINO! THIS NUMBER
INCLUDED JEWISH SOLDIERS THAT LEFT THEIR PROMISSED
LAND - PALESTINE - AND CONTINUED TO FIGHT IN EGYPT
AND ITALY.

5. There was one more Polish Army that was formed in May 1943 inside Russia. The "Union of Polish Patriots" (UPP) was founded through the invitation of the Polish communists. See Article entitled "Union of Polish Patriots."

It was controlled and directed by Stalin. From this the Kosciuszko 1st Polish Division was formed. The NKVD forced non-communist Poles to join. These were the unfortunate men who had been prevented from leaving Russia with the Anders evacuation to Iran. These Poles fought loyally alongside Soviet troops despite the suffering they had endured at Soviet hands in prisons or labor camps. They distinguished themselves in breaking through the last German lines of defense, the "POMERANIAN RAMPART" and also in the fighting at Saxony and in the capture of Berlin. The UPP became the foundation of the Communist Government created by the Soviets in Poland after World War II. The Polish soldiers who survived the war returned to live out their lives in Communist Poland.

Note: Our second cousin, Tadeusz Opalka, who by unfortunate circumstances, was separated in Siberia from his parents and siblings was forced to join this army. Once the war ended, he lived in Poland. Eventually he and his family emigrated to America.

EXPECTATION:

The Poles fought valiantly with the allies. So many lives were lost. All this was done with the expectation that Poland, once again, would be restored to be a free nation.

EXPECTATION SQUASHED: HISTORICAL FACTS/REALITY:
1.The Teheran Conference met in Iran.

In November 1943, President Roosevelt, Prime Minister Churchill, and Premier Stalin met in Teheran. This conference laid the foundation for what took place at the Yalta Conference.

2. The Yalta Conference met in Crimea.

In February 1945, the same leaders that met in Teheran met in Yalta a town in Crimea, on the Black Sea. All was implemented that Stalin demanded. He insisted that Poland be his Soviet Satellite. He promised free elections. The Allies gave him what he wanted. He soon broke his promise of free elections and a Communist Government was put in place in the newly named "Peoples Republic of Poland." See Article on Yalta Conference.

Winston Churchill, Franklin Roosevelt, and the man Roosevelt called "Uncle Joe."

The Yalta Conference took place February 4-11, 1945 at Yalta, Crimea between British Prime Minister Winston Churchill, U.S. President Franklin Delano Roosevelt, and Soviet Premier Joseph Stalin. Agreements reached included: 1) the demand for Germany's unconditional surrender 2) the establishment of a "provisional government of national unity" in Poland 3) a promise that the USSR would enter war against Japan 4) matters of the United Nations and other matters including those pertaining to Islands in Asia and the repatriation of Soviet citizens.

They agreed the Polish Lublin government supported by Stalin would undergo reorganization to broaden its base and include members of Poland's London government-in-exile. Stalin promised "free and unfettered elections based on universal suffrage and the secret ballot" in Poland as soon as possible. In addition, the Curzon line was accepted as the Polish-Soviet border. In essence, the Western Allies surrendered the center of Europe to the Soviets.

Stalin demanded that at the end of the war all Soviet citizens be repatriated to the Soviet Union whether they wanted to or not, and Churchill and Roosevelt agreed, unknowingly condemning many dissidents and old Russian exiles to death. In his book, "The Sword and the Shield," (former KGB employee) Mitrokhin writes (Basic Books 1999. page 134): "*In their desire to honor obligations to their ally, both the British and American governments collaborated in a sometimes barbarous repatriation....On June 1[in South Austria] battle-hardened soldiers of the 8th Argylls, some of them in tears, were ordered to break up a Cossack religious service and drive several thousands of unarmed men, women, and children into cattle trucks with rifle butts and pick handles. There were similar horrors on succeeding days. Some of the Cossacks killed themselves and their families to save them from torture, execution or the gulag.*"

3. The Potsdam Conference met near Berlin:

In July 1945, they again met, and Poland's borders were dramatically redrawn by the U. S., the U. K., and the U.S.S.R. It was called the "Curzon Line" and Poland lost 30,000 square miles of territory. The County of Lwow where we lived is presently part of the Ukraine and is spelled Lvov.

(Next see The New Borders of Poland article and map).

The **territorial changes of Poland after World War II** were very extensive.

The Second World War is usually dated from the German invasion of Poland, 1 September 1939. Both Britain and France had given guarantees to protect Poland from attack. Especially Stanisław Mikołajczyk insisted Britain had to keep its promise, and therefore he was forced to resign from the government-in-exile in November 1944. [1]

In 1945, Poland's borders were redrawn, following the decision taken at the Teheran Conference of 1943 at the insistence of the Soviet Union. The eastern Polish territories which the Soviet Union had occupied in 1939 (minus the Białystok region) were permanently annexed, and most of their Polish inhabitants expelled. Today these territories are part of Belarus, Ukraine and Lithuania.

Poland received former German territory east of the Oder-Neisse line in turn, consisting of the southern two thirds of East Prussia and most of Pomerania, Neumark (East Brandenburg), and Silesia. The German population was expelled before these "recovered territories" were repopulated with Poles from central Poland and those expelled from the eastern regions.

Polish resistance fighters were incarcerated or deported to Siberia by Stalin, in line with decisions forced upon Churchill and Roosevelt.

Poland's old and new borders, 1945

The fact that Western leaders tried to force Polish leaders to accept the conditions of Stalin is a matter of continuing resentment for some Poles even today. Some view it as a "betrayal" of Poland by the Western allies (which can be seen as part of a larger "betrayal" to allow it to fall entirely into the Soviet sphere of influence anyway). Moreover, it was used by ruling communists to underline anti-Western sentiments. It was easy to argue that Poland wasn't too important to the West, since its leaders sacrificed Poland's borders, legal government, and free elections.

Defenders of the actions taken by the Western allies maintain that realpolitik made it impossible to do anything else, and that they were in no shape to start a war with the Soviet Union over the subjugation

http://wapedia.mobi/en/Territorial_changes_of_Poland_after_World_War_II

The territorial changes of Poland after World War II were very extensive.

The Second World War is usually dated from the German invasion of Poland, 1 September 1939. Both Britain and France had given guarantees to protect Poland from attack. Especially Stanisław Mikołajczyk insisted Britain had to keep its promise, and therefore he was forced to resign from the government-in-exile in November 1944. [1]

In 1945, Poland's borders were redrawn, following the decision taken at the Teheran Conference of 1943 at the insistence of the Soviet Union. The eastern Polish territories which the Soviet Union had occupied in 1939 (minus the Bialystok region) were permanently annexed, and most of their Polish inhabitants expelled. Today these territories are part of Belarus, Ukraine and Lithuania.

Poland received former German territory east of the Oder-Neisse line in turn, consisting of the southern two thirds of East Prussia and most of Pomerania, Neumark (East Brandenburg), and Silesia. The German population was expelled before these "recovered territories" were repopulated with Poles from central Poland and those expelled from the eastern regions.

Polish resistance fighters were incarcerated or deported to Siberia by Stalin, in line with decisions forced upon Churchill and Roosevelt.

Poland's old and new borders, 1945

The fact that Western leaders tried to force Polish leaders to accept the conditions of Stalin is a matter of continuing resentment for some Poles even today. Some view it as a "betrayal" of Poland by the Western allies (which can be seen as part of a larger "betrayal" to allow it to fall entirely into the Soviet sphere of influence anyway). Moreover, it was used by ruling communists to underline anti-Western sentiments. It was easy to argue that Poland wasn't too important to the West, since its leaders sacrificed Poland's borders, legal government, and free elections.

Defenders of the actions taken by the Western allies maintain that realpolitik made it impossible to do anything else, and that they were in no shape to start a war with the Soviet Union over the subjugation

http://wapedia.mobi/en/Territorial_changes_of_Poland_after_World_War_II

Poland was sold out by the U.S. and the U.K.!

From an article entitled: "They Did Not Teach Me This in School." "The circumstances of the odyssey and tragic history of Polish Citizens under occupation during the war (WWII) was hushed up by the Allies during the war to protect the reputation of the Soviet Union, who was an ally against the Nazis. WE (Poles) were not only deported from our land but also deported from history!"

My Note: It is true–you cannot find anything that happened to us in any history books!

WWII ended May 8, 1945. Japan signed surrender terms on September 2, 1945 on the U.S.S. Missouri in Tokyo Bay.

At some point the survivors of the Anders Army were shipped from Italy to England. Dad's Military Service ended on January 28, 1947. He was discharged officially on January 28, 1949.
(See Discharge Papers).

How my family suffered by the effects of WWII is only a part of the horrible suffering of millions of people of many nationalities! 50 million lives were lost from so many countries. How many Polish lives were lost! An estimated 20 million (16,825,000) people died in Europe, over 15% of Europe's population (internet). Worldwide over 60 million people died because of this war! (internet). We survivors are grateful and thankful to the military allies who fought the evil AXIS countries and gave their lives to bring an end to World War II!

It becomes totally overwhelming to try to understand the scope of WWII and of the atrocities committed just because of the desire of a few insane men who wanted to rule supreme over other countries!

Note!
Menachem Begin (Aug. 16, 1913 to March 9, 1992).
Born in the Russian Empire (today Brest, Belarus). He became a member of the Zionist Movement. He eventually became the Sixth Prime Minister of Israel.

At 14, he was sent to a Polish Government School. Then he began his studies in "law" at the University of Poland.

He was sent to Russia with primarily the Polish people when we were freed. Begin joined the Free Anders Army that my father was also a part of. He and other Poles eventually were sent to Palestine in May 1942.
See Picture of Menachem Begin.

Menachem Begin (Hebrew: מְנַחֵם בֵּגִין *Menaḥem Begin*

Polish: *Mieczysław Biegun*; Russian: Менахем Вольфович Бегин *Menakhem Volfovich Begin*; 16 August 1913 – 9 March 1992) was an Israeli politician, founder of Likud and the sixth Prime Minister of Israel. Before the creation of the state of Israel, he was the leader of the Zionist militant group Irgun, the Revisionist breakaway from the larger Jewish paramilitary organization Haganah. He proclaimed a revolt, on 1 February 1944, against the British mandatory government, which was opposed by the Jewish Agency. As head of the Irgun, he targeted the British in Palestine.[1] Later, the Irgun fought the Arabs during the 1947–48 Civil War in Mandatory Palestine.

Begin was elected to the first Knesset, as head of Herut, the party he founded, and was at first on the political fringe, embodying the opposition to the Mapai-led government and Israeli establishment. He remained in opposition in the eight consecutive elections (except for a national unity government around the Six-

Menachem Begin

מנחם בגין

HEAD PAGES 4-8

4.

Menachem Begin was born to Zeev Dov and Hassia Biegun in what was then Brest-Litovsk in the Russian Empire (today Brest, Belarus). He was the youngest of three children.[4] On his mother's side he was descended from distinguished rabbis. His father, a timber merchant, was a community leader, a passionate Zionist, and an admirer of Theodor Herzl. The midwife who attended his birth was the grandmother of Ariel Sharon.[5]

After a year of a traditional cheder education Begin started studying at a "Tachkemoni" school, associated with the religious Zionist movement. In his childhood, Begin, like most Jewish children in his town, was a member of the Zionist scouts movement Hashomer Hatzair. He was a member of Hashomer Hatzair until the age of 13, and at 16, he joined Betar.[6] At 14, he was sent to a Polish government school,[7] where he received a solid grounding in classical literature.

Begin studied law at the University of Warsaw, where he learned the oratory and rhetoric skills that became his trademark as a politician, and viewed as demagogy by his critics.[8] During his studies, he organized a self-defense group of Jewish students to counter harassment by anti-Semites on campus.[9] He graduated in 1935, but never practiced law. At this time he became a disciple of Vladimir "Ze'ev" Jabotinsky, the founder of the nationalist Revisionist Zionism movement and its youth wing, Betar.[10] His rise within Betar was

See Poland's Story from Russian communism to a free Poland!
Biography of Lech Walesa and picture.

POLAND'S STORY from Russian Communism to a free Poland!

Lech Walesa
The Nobel Peace Prize 1983

Biography

Lech Walesa was born on September 29, 1943 in Popowo, Poland. After graduating from vocational school, he worked as a car mechanic at a machine center from 1961 to 1965. He served in the army for two years, rose to the rank of corporal, and in 1967 was employed in the Gdansk shipyards as an electrician. In 1969 he married Danuta Golos and they have eight children.

During the clash in December 1970 between the workers and the government, he was one of the leaders of the shipyard workers and was briefly detained. In 1976, however, as a result of his activities as a shop steward, he was fired and had to earn his living by taking temporary jobs.

In 1978 with other activists he began to organise free non-communist trade unions and took part in many actions on the sea coast. He was kept under surveillance by the state security service and frequently detained.

In August 1980 he led the Gdansk shipyard strike which gave rise to a wave of strikes over much of the country with Walesa seen as the leader. The primary demands were for workers' rights. The authorities were forced to capitulate and to negotiate with Walesa the Gdansk Agreement of August 31, 1980, which gave the workers the right to strike and to organise their own independent union.

The Catholic Church supported the movement, and in January 1981 Walesa was cordially received by Pope John Paul II in the Vatican. Walesa himself has always regarded his Catholicism as a source of strength and inspiration. In the years 1980-81 Walesa travelled to Italy, Japan, Sweden, France and Switzerland as guest of the International Labour Organisation. In September 1981 he was elected Solidarity Chairman at the First National Solidarity Congress in Gdansk.

The country's brief enjoyment of relative freedom ended in December 1981, when General Jaruzelski, fearing Soviet armed intervention among other considerations, imposed martial law, "suspended" Solidarity, arrested many of its leaders, and interned Walesa in a country house in a remote spot.

In November 1982 Walesa was released and reinstated at the Gdansk shipyards. Although kept under surveillance, he managed to maintain lively contact with Solidarity leaders in the underground. While martial law was lifted in July 1983, many of the restrictions were continued in civil code. In October 1983 the announcement of Walesa's Nobel prize raised the spirits of the underground movement, but the award was attacked by the government press.

The Jaruzelski regime became even more unpopular as economic conditions worsened, and it was finally forced to negotiate with Walesa and his Solidarity colleagues. The result was the holding of parliamentary elections which, although limited, led to the establishment of a non-communist government. Under Mikhail Gorbachev the Soviet Union was no longer prepared to use military force to keep communist parties in satellite states in power.

Walesa, now head of the revived Solidarity labour union, began a series of meetings with world leaders.

In April 1990 at Solidarity's second national congress, Walesa was elected chairman with 77.5% of the votes. In December 1990 in a general ballot he was elected President of the Republic of Poland. He served until defeated in the election of November 1995.

Walesa has been granted many honorary degrees from universities, including Harvard University and the University of Paris. Other honors include the Medal of Freedom (Philadelphia, U.S.A.); the Award of Free World (Norway); and the European Award of Human Rights.

Selected Bibliography

By Walesa

The Struggle and the Triumph. New York: Arcade, 1992.

A Way of Hope. New York: Henry Holt, 1987.

Other Sources

Craig, Mary. *Lech Walesa and His Poland.* New York: Continuum, 1987. (By a popular writer who knows Poland well. Based on extensive research and interviews with Walesa and others. Covers the period through 1986. Highly recommended.)

Goodwyn, Lawrence. *Breaking the Barrier: The Rise of Solidarity in Poland.* New York: Oxford University Press, 1991.

Kurski, Jaroslaw. *Lech Walesa: Democrat or Dictator.* Boulder, Colorado: Westview Press, 1993. (Translated by Peter Obst. The period July 1989 to March 1992. By Walesa's press spokesman, whose purpose is "to portray Lech in motion".)

From *Nobel Lectures, Peace 1981-1990*, Editor-in-Charge Tore Frängsmyr, Editor Irwin Abrams, World Scientific Publishing Co., Singapore, 1997

This autobiography/biography was first published in the book series *Les Prix Nobel*. It was later edited and republished in *Nobel Lectures*. To cite this document, always state the source as shown above.

The Story of England is next.

A
NEW
BEGINNING

ENGLAND

England:

(Refer to map of United Kingdom)

Father with the Anders Army left Italy and already was in England for some time. Mom, Zofia, and I left Tanganyika and sailed into Liverpool on April 2, 1948. Zdzislaw and Antoni arrived in Liverpool shortly before us. (Refer to Large Map)

(For Dad follow #4C –Italy to #6 England) Very first map.

(For us from #5 Tanganyika to #6 England) Very first map.

We were taken to a transitional camp in Hartford Bridge. We were given lodging in barracks. Each barrack was lined with beds on both sides to accommodate women, their daughters, and sons. There were no partitions. We ate at a community dining room. We must have been there quite some time as I enclose a photo that we had religious processions there.

Dad when he was released from the Army eventually joined us in Hartford Bridge. What a joyous occasion it was to finally have him with us after over five years of separation.

A beautiful young girl, Zofia's age, Eugenia (Gienia) Rosa became very attached to us on the ship ORBITA. Her mother had died in Uzbekistan. She had been in the orphanage in Camp Tengeru because her father and older brother were in the Anders Army. She was sailing to be reunited with them. When we were in Harford Bridge, she became part of our family until her father came for her.   She is now 86 and lives with her husband in Doylestown, PA. She told me she walks 2 ½ miles each day and still enjoys dancing. (From a Conversation in June 2015).

The single discharged Polish soldiers as well as the young Polish girls both were anxious to meet each other, to date and to have some fun as did Zofia and Gienia. While working as a waitress in Hartford Bridge, Zofia met her future husband, Wladyslaw Englert. He was a very distinguished soldier in the Polish Army and received many medals. But soon after this meeting our family was relocated to our permanent location in Morpeth.

Our Address Was:

43B Common Camp

Morpeth, Northumberland

We lived in barracks as before but this time we had privacy. Our family of six was given half a barrack all to ourselves. For the first time, truly, we were living in a modern society. There were community showers and, at first, a community dining hall. The barracks had electricity for lighting, a coal stove, a sink with running water but best of all we had a private flushing toilet! There were two bedrooms and a kitchen/living room. Our barrack was the last one in the camp and faced a large open field. We could see a golf course on the right. When we walked or biked on this field to go to Morpeth we saw fields of Brussel Sprouts growing to the left. Then passing by a cemetery (for the longest time I had bad dreams about this cemetery) we entered the outskirts of Morpeth which was a very charming town (Postcard enclosed). The castle on the right had become a Police Station and on the opposite side was a park with a beautiful garden. Once in a while (being there at the right time) we were entertained by bagpipe music (it sounded strange) and Scotts in kilts dancing around swords laid down in the form of a cross. This was a novelty for us to experience.

Dad and Zdzislaw (Age 16) got work at an "open coal mine" located a few miles past Morpeth. The industry of coal mining was huge. A large city we visited occasionally was Newcastle-On-Tyne. At that time, it was an export center of coal. It also was the County Seat of NORTHUMBERLAND. Zofia got a job at a bakery. Antoni was sent to school in southern England. I went to school in Morpeth. It was a Catholic School named St. Robert's.

I was 9 ½. I did very poorly in school. We all struggled to learn the new language. Mom worked hard taking care of her large family.

The enormous cost of WWII in lives and treasure, the destruction of some cities and infrastructure by German bombs took a great toll on Great Britain. One major consequence was the rationing of food for all its people. Resourceful as my parents were and because of our location in the camp, we had space to grow our own vegetables. Also, Dad and the boys raised chickens primarily for eggs. This was a great help in feeding our family. Yet we still had to rely on purchases made in Morpeth. I remember Zofia telling us this story: She or my brothers were sent to Morpeth's butcher shop to buy bones for soup. It was their only purchase. At times when the butcher saw them come in, he would shout "No more bones today!" This did not bother my brothers, but Zofia was extremely embarrassed by this loud call out!

I broke a leg bone while playing hopscotch at school. All expenses were paid by the newly established socialized medicine.

Wladyslaw Englert came to our camp looking for Zofia after their initial meeting in Hartford Bridge. He courted my sister and on July 16, 1949, Zofia, age 20, married Wladyslaw, age 28, at St. Robert's Catholic Church, Morpeth. See photo of Zofia's marriage. Notice that Antoni is missing as he was away in school. Zofia and Wladyslaw really liked living in England. They liked the dress of England and their formal ways.

MORPETH - SMALL CITY CLOSEST TO OUR "COMMON CAMP"

ZOFIA & WLADYSLAW ENGLERT - WEDDING 1949
ZDISLAW - BACK ROW ; JAN, KATARZYNA & HELENA
RODZINA   MORPETH, ENGLAND

KATARZYNA , HELENA , ZOFIA   ANTONI - ZDZISLAW
            ENGLERT
        MORPETH , ENGLAND - 1950

1949 - HARTFORD BRIDGE / BEDLINGTON , ENGLAND

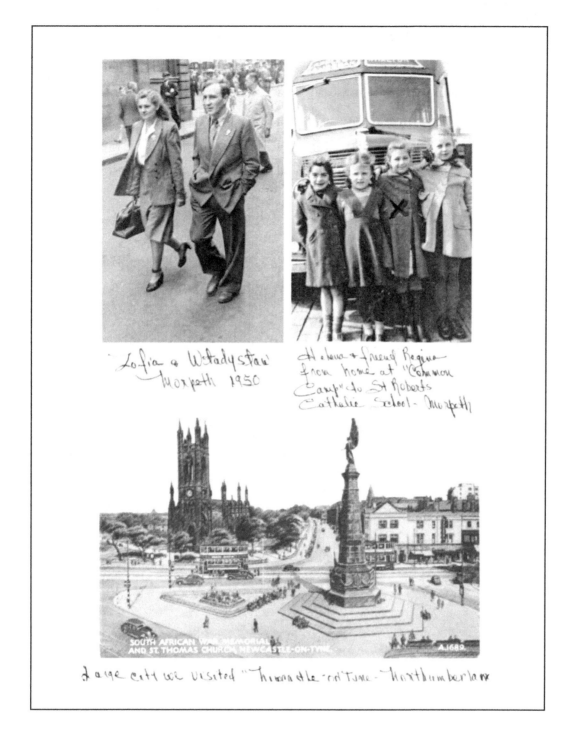

Zofia & Władysław
Morpeth 1950

Helena & friend Regina
from home at "Common
Camp" to St Roberts
Catholic School - Morpeth

SOUTH AFRICAN WAR MEMORIAL
AND ST. THOMAS CHURCH, NEWCASTLE-ON-TYNE.   A.1689

Large city we visited "Newcastle-on-Tyne - Northumberland

Whenever possible my brothers and I went to Morpeth to view Hollywood movies. They looked forward to the Westerns and the war movies, typical of all boys! I looked forward to Esther Williams and Jane Powell movies and immersed myself in a fantasy world. Also, for the first time I tasted ice cream and wiggly jello. Both were delicious. I tasted my first black licorice and Brussel sprouts, and I didn't like them at all!

My parents were very unhappy that Zdzislaw, at such a young age, was working in a coal mine. Once Antoni returned from school in the south, both boys were enrolled in an Agricultural School in Glasgow, Scotland.

(See Certificate). They completed one year of study.

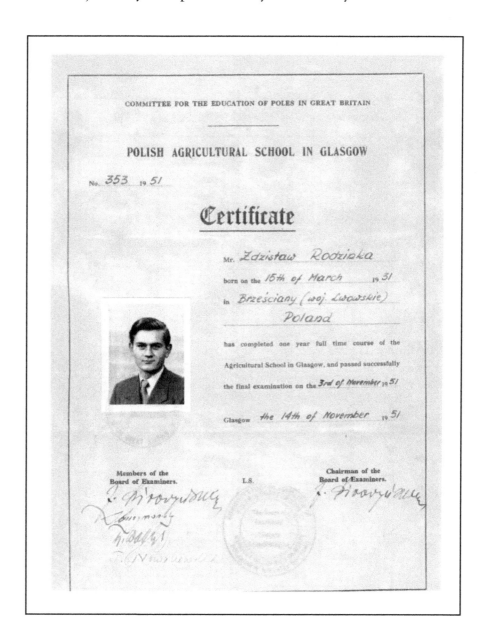

The following table shows the standard achieved in the subjects of the School by

Mr. *Zdzisław Rodzinka*

No.	Subject	Mark
1	Religious knowledge	Very good
2	Polish	Fair
3	English	Fair
4	History and Geography	Good
5	Mathematics	Good
6	Natural science	Good
7	Surveying and Rural Architecture	Good
8	Forestry	Good
9	Plants production	Fair
10	Animal husbandry	Fair
11	Farm Management and Applied Book-keeping	Good
12	Horticulture	Fair
13	Practical work	Very good
14		
15		
16		

L.S.

Headmaster :

Things were quite good for us. We were on our way to becoming integrated and assimilated into British society.

Then in 1950 an Immigration Quota was established by the U.S., allowing 17,000 former Polish Soldiers and their families to immigrate to America. We needed a sponsor who would assure the government that he would offer a home and job opportunity for the adults. Mom's brother Jan Grzasko sponsored us as well as Wladyslaw and Zofia.

Uncle Jan came to America from Poland as a young man well before WWII. He married Agnes Drejza and had two daughters Frances and Clarise. They owned a grocery store on Martin Street in Utica, N.Y. Note: Mom's brother Franek and her sister Maria also came to America at a very young age. Both made their homes in the Detroit area.

The following are exhibits all pertaining to our travelling to America:

Sponsor document

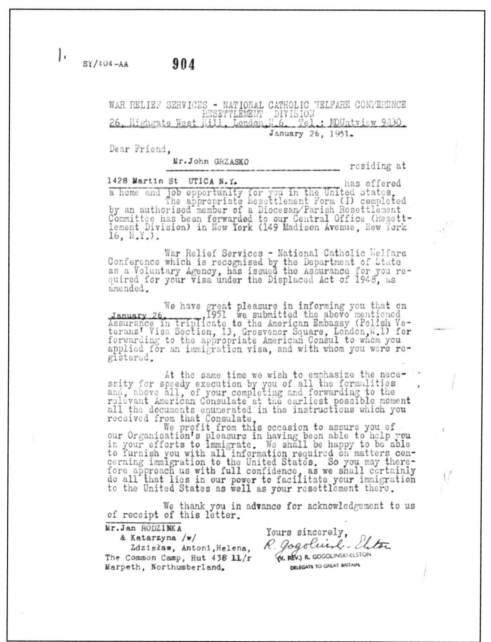

See Letter Oct. 15, 1951 –Visa still valid.

PP:SC

THE FOREIGN SERVICE
OF THE
UNITED STATES OF AMERICA

ADDRESS OFFICIAL COMMUNICATIONS TO

American Consulate,
53, Huskisson Street,
Liverpool, England.
October 15, 1951.

Mr. Jan Rodzinka,
43 B, Common Camp,
Morpeth,
Northumberland.

Sir:

Receipt is acknowledged of your letter dated
October 12, 1951, regarding your immigration visa.

As you are sailing on November 13, your visa
will still be valid. If, however, you do not sail
on that date, you must obtain replacement visas.
You and your family will be called for further applications and this office, and you must furnish 3
more photographs for each member of your family, have
another medical examination, and pay for each visa.

You should inform this office if you require such
visas.

Very truly yours,

Paul Plenni
American Vice Consul

See Letter November 17, 1951–sea passage ticket on the Mauretania.

GA/JH.

3,

REGISTERED

MINISTRY OF LABOUR AND NATIONAL SERVICE

MUSeum 1577
Ext. 522

Central Polish Resettlement Office,
24/25 Cumberland Terrace,
Regent's Park,
London, N. W. 1.

Ref. E.M.P. 2336/51.

17 No. 1951

Dear Sir/Madam,

With reference to the passage booked for you on ss/mv
"MAURETANIA"   due to sail on   13th November, 1951,
from   Southampton   to   New York,
please find enclosed:-

1. Sea passage ticket,
    xxxxxxxxxxxxxxxxxxxxxxxxxxxxxxxxxxxxxxxxxxxxxx
    xxxxxxxxxxxxxxxxxxxxxxxxxxxxxxxxxxxxxxxxxxxxxx
    xxxxxxxxxxxxxxx

2. Seat reservation for boat train from London to port of embarkation,

3. Railway ticket(s) from   New York   to   Utica, N.Y., U.S.A.

4. Railway warrant(s) from   ----   to   ----

5. _____   ----

6. Form of receipt for documents listed above; this should be signed
    and returned to this Office without delay.

7. Embarkation Card(s) I.B.29 which must be completed and, signed by
    each non-British passenger and handed to the immigration authorities
    on embarkation/xxxxxxxxxxxxxxxxxxxxx.

8. Supply of baggage labels, instructions concerning baggage,
    insurance, etc.

                                                    is enclosed
    Embarkation Notice which must be strictly observed   will follow

        Please note that the following documents will have to be
surrendered to H.M. Immigration Officers on embarkation:-
Ration Book, National Registration Identity Card, Medical Card, and
Police Certificate of Registration.

                        Yours faithfully,

P.1(30/3)

Mr. Jan RODZINKA,
    43 B., Morpeth Common Camp,
        Morpeth,
            Northumberland

New York Passenger Lists, 1820-1957

New York Passenger Lists, 1820-1957

Name:	Helen Rodzimka
Arrival Date:	19 Nov 1951
Estimated Birth Year:	abt 1940
Age:	11
Gender:	Female
Port of Departure:	Southampton
Place of Origin:	Stateless
Ship Name:	Mauretania
Search Ship Database:	Search the Mauretania in the 'Passenger Ships and Images' database
Port of Arrival:	New York, New York
Line:	13
Microfilm Serial:	T715
Microfilm Roll:	T715_8067
Page Number:	68

Source Citation: Year: 1951; Microfilm serial: T715; Microfilm roll: T715_8067; Line: 13; .

Source Information:
Ancestry.com. *New York Passenger Lists, 1820-1957* [database on-line]. Provo, UT, USA: The Generations Network, Inc., 2006. Original data:

- Passenger Lists of Vessels Arriving at New York, New York, 1820-1897; (National Archives Microfilm Publication M237, 675 rolls); Records of the U.S. Customs Service, Record Group 36; National Archives, Washington, D.C.

- Passenger and Crew Lists of Vessels Arriving at New York, New York, 1897-1957; (National Archives Microfilm Publication T715, 8892 rolls); Records of the Immigration and Naturalization Service; National Archives, Washington, D.C.

Description:
This database is an index to the passenger lists of ships arriving from foreign ports at the port of New York from 1820-1957. In addition, the names found in the index are linked to actual images of the passenger lists. Information contained in the index includes given name, surname, age, gender, arrival date, port of arrival, port of departure and ship name. Learn more...

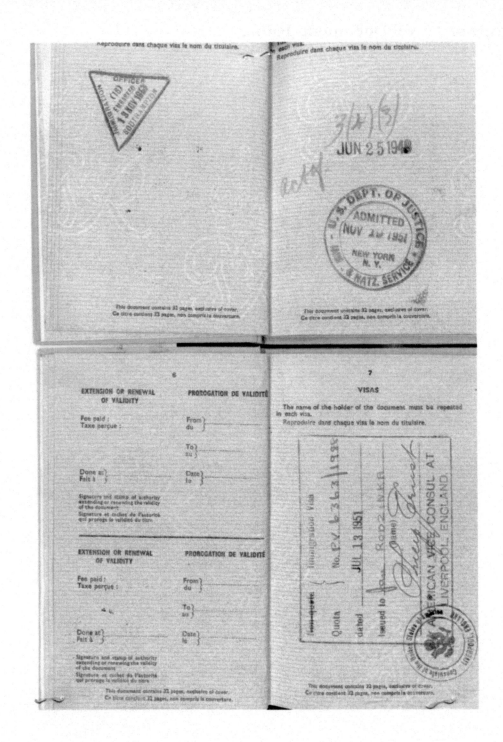

See Copy of Travel Document– Mother

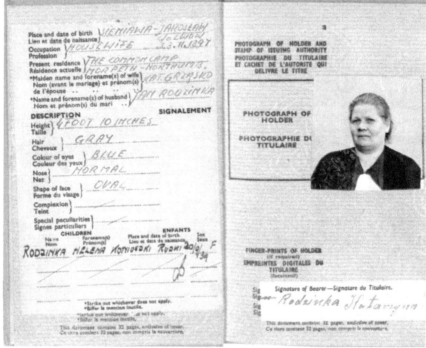

See Photo of ship Mauretania

CUNARD WHITE STAR R. M. S. MAURETANIA.

from SOUTHAMPTON NOU 13 to N.Y. City NOU 19, 1951
Dad, Mom, Zdsistaw, Antoni & Helena

Mauretania

Ship Information

Ship Name:	Mauretania
Years in service:	1939-
Funnels:	2
Masts:	2
Shipping Line:	Cunard
Ship Description:	Built by Cammell, Laird & Co., Ltd., Birkenhead, England. Tonnage: 35,738. Dimensions: 739' x 89' (771' o.l.). Twin-screw, 22 1/2 knots. Steam turbines. Two masts and two funnels.
History:	Launched, July 28, 1938. Maiden voyage: Liverpool-New York, June 17, 1939. Made just two voyages to New York before World War II. Employed as a troopship during the war. Resumed trans-Atlantic service in April 1947. Passengers: 470 first, 370 cabin, 300 tourist (as of 1960). Ports: Southampton-Havre-Cobh-New York. Crew of 600 members.

MANIFEST OF IN-BOUND PASSNGERS (ALIENS)

arriving at port of 19 Nov N.YORK

STATELESS

EXEMPT

Mauretanias Ship Log

```
Jan Rodzinka     A. 8176335—ALIEN REGISTRATION
Born: August 13, 1899                        NUMBER
pow. Sanok, woj. Lwow
POLAND


Katarzyna Rodzinka    A. 8176336
Born: November 23, 1897
pow. Jaroslaw, woj. Lwow
POLAND


Sophie Englert- naturalized citizen-no. 7123862
Born: May 13, 1929
pow. Sambor, woj. Lwow
POLAND


Zdzislaw Rodzinka              ANTONI RODZINKA
Born: March 15, 1932           BORN: JUNE 9, 1934
pow. Sambor, woj. Lwow         pow: SAMBOR
POLAND                         woj. LWOW

                                  POLAND
Helen Rodzinka    A. 8176339
Born: September 20, 1939
pow. Rudki, woj. Lwow
POLAND


Janina Dolega
Born: November 25, 1926
pow. Sambor, woj. Lwow
POLAND


Address in Africa.
     Polish Refuges Camp
     Tengeru via Arusha
     Tanganyika


Address in England
     43 B  Common Camp
Morpeth, Northumberland


        Powjat - County
        Wojewutstwo - Province
```

Dec. 24, 1951 First Christmas in U.S.
Helena, Dad, Wladyslaw, Richard, Zofia Englerta Man.

Sept. 1952 w/Uncle John
sister Mary from Detroit
& our parents.

Antoni, Wladyslaw, Zdzislawa Helena
Dec. 24 1951 @ Uncle John's house

Spring of 1952 - Englerts apt @ Burstone Rd.

1952 - our Apartment
@ 54 Floyd St. N.Y. Mills.

158 MAIN ST. N.Y. MILLS, N.Y.

House we Purchased

Helena, Antoni, Richard & Mom & Dad.
1954 Inside our House

Dad - on our own Property

Jan & Katarzyna - our Parents

The Englert's sailed out of England on the Queen Elizabeth a number of months before us. Zofia was pregnant. Our family boarded the ship, Mauretania, at Southampton and arrived 6 days later at New York City. It was November 19, 1951.

My family did not know how our lives would turn out in America; but we were certain that we would be much better than what we had endured in the past. When the Englert's arrived in Utica they lived with Uncle John (Jan).

Once they found jobs, they rented an apartment on Burrstone Road in N.Y. Mills, N.Y. Their son Richard was born on August 31, 1951. When we arrived Uncle John had already rented and furnished an apartment for the 5 of us at 59 Floyd St., N.Y. Mills, N.Y. The majority of the people in this village were of Polish decent and spoke Polish. For example: Polish Church, 2 bakeries, doctor, dentist, gas station owner and some people in the village government spoke Polish.

Our first Thanksgiving and Christmas were celebrated at Uncle John and Aunt Agnes's home. My parents were incredibly grateful for the many ways that they extended themselves to bring us to this country. They continued aiding our family until such a time as we became self-sufficient. To this day we are thankful for their kindness. With appreciation and gratitude, we honor their memory.

We permanently settled in the village of New York Mills, New York. My Dad quickly obtained a job at a Polish owned bakery: Bazan Bakery, Utica. I was enrolled at St. Mary's School which was part of St. Mary's Catholic Church. The Nuns spoke Polish. This enabled me to do well in school. Zdzislaw's first job was with "Dunlop Tire company. It was full time. He performed various jobs. He stated that the work was very hard.

Antoni worked at Uncle John's grocery store on Martin Ave, Utica. It was part-time so Uncle John's brother-in-law offered him a job as a maintenance man.

We eventually bought another house in the village which had a large lot. This allowed Mom to have a large vegetable garden plus a flower garden including her favorite rose bushes.

Yet this was not enough for my brothers. Antoni enlisted in the U.S. Air Force. One of the places he was stationed at was Iceland. Zdzislaw enlisted in the U.S. Navy and was stationed in the Caribbean Sea. When they became American Citizens, they both embraced American Names: Tony and Jess.

After Tony left the service, Tony with three other friends decided to follow the words of Horace Greeley, an American journalist and politician (1811-1872) who said, "Go west young man! Go west!" So, they did and ended up in Los Angeles, California. They did not find it easy working there and especially being away from the family. When my Dad died Tony came home and settled here. He married Dorothy and bought a home in Yorkville. They had two sons: Michael and Mark.

Shortly after my Father's death, Jess, who stayed with us, decided to seek his fortune elsewhere. I took him to the train station in Utica and he went to California. He made his home in the Los Angeles area. He confessed that it was difficult for him there. But he met a girl named Marcella. They married and had a son Rick. They also had two children by Marcella's first marriage. They made their home in Hawthorne and still live there. We are frequently in touch.

My parents also attended classes for citizenship. Both received this great privilege shortly after being here in the U.S. a little over 5 years. Both kept their original names.

I, Helena, received my citizenship document at the age of 19. I, like my brothers, embraced a new name: Helen!

One thing we were incredibly grateful for was my sister Zofia (who became Sophie in America.) Her talents were sewing, knitting, and crocheting and she was extremely helpful to us as we entered out new life in America.

Still our family was not complete as one member was missing– "Janina"! She was separated from us since December 1939. Because of unfortunate circumstances she had been left behind in Poland.

Dec. 24, 1951 First Christmas in U.S.
Helena, Dad, Władysław, Richard, Zofia Englerta mom.

Sept. 1952 w/ Uncle John
Sister Mary from Detroit
+ our Parents.

Antoni, Władysław, Zdzisława Helena
Dec. 24, 1951 @ Uncle John's House

Spring of 1952 - Englerts Apt. @ Burstone Rd.

1952 - our Apartment
@ 54 Floyd St. N.Y. Mills

158 MAIN ST. N.Y. MILLS, N.Y.

HOUSE WE PURCHASED

Helena, Antoni, Richard & Mom & Dad.
1954 INSIDE OUR HOUSE

DAD. ON OUR OWN PROPERTY

JAN & KATARZYNA - OUR PARENTS

I briefly tell her story.

POLAND
JANINA'S
STORY

POLAND'S NEW BORDERS AFTER 1945

Aunt Aniela & Janina

Zosia, Janina & Father Sienko

Janina 1935?

November 1946

Zosia & Janina

POLAND 1953

ALOJZY & JANINA (RODZINKA) DOLĘGA
OSTROWICE POLAND   SEPT 17, 1946

Janina, Alojzy, Dionha,
Krystyna & Ryszard

back row: JANINA (RODZINKA)   Front: Dionia; her mom - our aunt
and husband ALOJZY DOLĘGA   Aniela Stopusielowicz;
aunt JADWIGA GRZĄSKO   KRYSTYNA DOLĘGA; bride & groom -
uncle STANISŁAW GRZĄSKO   HELENA & EDWARD GRZĄSKO; DIONIZA;
                               aunt WIKTORIA GRZĄSKO - ED's mom & RYSZARD

Janina's Story

In December 1939, our sister, Janina was sent to Aunt Aniela Lopusiewicz because we had been robbed and lacked many things. In February 1940, while we were deported to Siberia, Russia, Aunt Aniela and her family including Janina were not. Janina remained in Aniela's care while the war was all around them in Poland. She also lived with Aunt Jadwiga in Sambor. With the end of WWII, Janina attended business school and obtained a job as manager of a store.

I imagine that life was difficult for our sister—without parents, with the devastation that had been left behind in Poland by the war—and then living under communism.

Janina met Alojzy Dolega, and they married on December 26, 1945, at OSTROWICE. They had three children:
Ryszard–October 16, 1946
Krystyna–January 5, 1948
Dioniza–January 12, 1950

Approximately 10 years after we arrived in America, my parents and Alojzy's brother Raymond (who lived in Syracuse) sponsored Janina and her family to immigrate to America. At that time, they were living in the city of LEGNICA.

In 1961 Janina, Alojzy, and their children sailed from GDANSK to the PORT of MONTREAL, Canada. Zdzislaw and Raymond drove to Montreal to pick them up. Finally, after 20 years of separation we were finally reunited with the exception of Antoni who was living in California. It was an incredibly happy occasion to be reunited with Janina and to meet her family!

Alojzy got a job at Hapanowicz Market as he was a great butcher. Janina worked at Mele Manufacturing Company. The children were very bright and attended school in Utica. They did well in school.

Eventually the Dolega family moved to HAMTRAMCK, Detroit, an area which had a large Polish community. Mother's sister Mary and brother Frank also lived in the Detroit area.

Janina and Alojzy worked hard and did well for themselves and for their children who prospered in this country called America!

Documents for the Dolega Family:

See Affidavit of Support

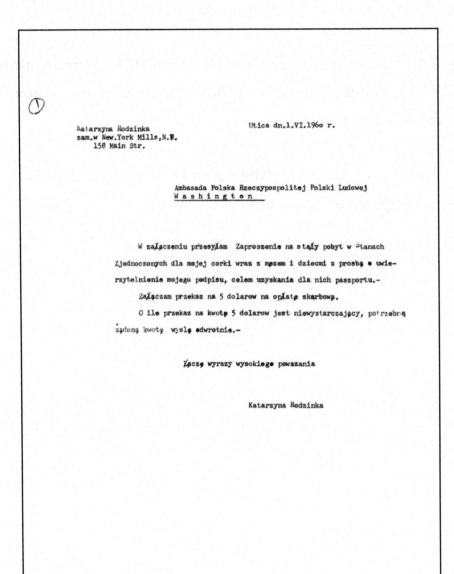

Katarzyna Rodzinka   Utica dn.1.VI.1960 r.
zam.w New.York Mills,N.Y.
     158 Main Str.

                    Ambasada Polska Rzeczypospolitej Polski Ludowej
                    W a s h i n g t o n

          W załączeniu przesyłam Zaproszenie na stały pobyt w Stanach
     Zjednoczonych dla mojej corki wraz z mężem i dziecmi z prosbą o uwie-
     rzytelnienie mojego podpisu, celem uzyskania dla nich paszportu.-
          Załączam przekaz na 5 dolarow na opłatę skarbowę.
          O ile przekaz na kwotę 5 dolarow jest niewystarczający, potrzebną
     żądaną kwotę wyslę odwrotnie.-

                    Łączę wyrazy wysokiego powazania

                         Katarzyna Rodzinka

utica 1.czerwca 1960 r.

Z A P R O S Z E N I E

Zapraszam moją corkę Janinę Rodzinka DOŁĘGĘ ,urodzoną 23 Listopada 1927 r
w Brzescianach powiat Sambor, corkę Jana i Katarzyny Grzasko, jej męża
Alojzego DOŁĘGĘ, urodz.21 Czerwca 1912 r. w Wolicy powiat Sambor, syna Antoniego
i Zofii z domu Gurak, oraz ich dzieci :

1) syn Ryszard, urodz. 16 Listopada 1946 r.

2) corka Krystyna Marię, urodz.5 Stycznia 1948 r.

3) corka Deodysa weronika, urodz. 12 Stycznia 1950 r.

wszyscy obecnie zamieszkali w Legnicy, przy ul.Rewolucji Październikowej
L.61 ojew.Wrocław, na s t a ł y   p o b y t   w Stanach Zjednoczonych.

Wszelkie koszta wynikłe z ich przyjazdem, oraz pobytem w Stanach
Zjednoczonych będą pokryte z moich funduszów.

Katarzyna Rodzinka
zamieszkała w New York Mills, N.Y.
158 Main Str.

See Above Notice of Approval of Visa Petition.

(3)

United States of America

County of Oneida
SS
June 2/57
1-133-Aire
State of NY NY

Affidavit of Support

Katarzyna Rodzinka   residing at 158 Main St.
(Name)   (Street Address)

NY Mils   NY, being duly sworn depose and say:
(City)   (State)

1. That I am a native born citizen of the United States having been born in the	That I became a naturalized citizen of the United States on:	That I declared my intention of becoming a citizen of the United States on:
City of	Date May 9/57 In the	Date In the
State of	Rome Oneida (City) (County) NY (State) number	(City) (County) (State) number
	of my certificate being 7456028	of my certificate being
	issued by the Court of Supreme	issued by the Court of

2. That I was born in Sieniowa Yoroslaw Poland   Date Nov. 23-1897

3. That it is my (our) intention and desire to have my (our) relatives (friends) whose names appear below, at present residing at:

ul Rewolucji Pazdziernikowej
(Give complete address)
Nr 41, III Legnica Poland

come to the United States for permanent residence.

Name of Alien	Sex	Date of Birth	Country of Birth	Occupation	Relationship to Deponent
Janina Rodzinka Dolega	F	Nov 23/27	Poland	force clerk Manager	Daughter
Alojzy Dolega	M	Jan 4/1912	Poland	Butcher	son-in-law
Ryszard	M	Oct 16/44	Poland	student	grand-son
Krystyna Maria	F	Jan	Poland	student	grand daughter
Jadwiga Wernika	F	Judy	Poland	student	grand "

4. That my regular occupation is Ownership — Meatland Employed by
(Business Name and Address)
White Eagle Bakery, 1110 Lincoln Ave, Utica NY.

and my average earnings amount to $4,160.00 per year —

5. That I (We) possess the following financial assets of which corroborative evidence is herewith attached:

Savings Account # ___ in The Savings Bank of Utica
Owner of Property at 158 Main St. New York Mils
assessed value $10,000

6. That my (our) dependents consist of 0 dependents 1 daughter (17)

That I (We) am (are) willing and able to receive, maintain, support the alien (s) after their immigration to the United States, and hereby assume such obligations guaranteeing that none of them will at any time become public charges upon any community in the United States; and that any of school age will be sent to school.

That this affidavit is made by me (us) voluntarily and of my (our) free will in order that our American Consul will issue visas to the above mentioned relatives (friends) so that they may enter the United States for permanent residence.

SWORN TO BEFORE ME THIS
_____

_____ DAY OF _____ 195___   _____

UNITED STATES DEPARTMENT OF JUSTICE
Immigration and Naturalization Service

NOTICE OF APPROVAL OF VISA PETITION

U.S. Post Office Bldg.
Albany, New York

Date: **November 12, 1958**

File No.: **VP 07-I-21647**

Mrs. Katarzyna Rodzinka
158 Main Street
New York Mills
New York

Re: Janina Rodzinka Dolega, daughter

Dear Madam:

Your Visa Petition has been approved by this Service and forwarded to the appropriate American Consul. The actual issuance of visas is a function of American Consular officers who serve under the Visa Division of the Department of State. The American Consular officer having jurisdiction over the place where the intended beneficiary resides will notify him as soon as the approved petition is received and inform him of all further steps necessary to apply for a visa. It is unnecessary for you or the prospective beneficiary to take any further action until receipt of appropriate notice from the American Consular office.

Sincerely yours,

CHAS. H. WITHERS, JR.
Officer in Charge

Att.

P.S. You have indicated on Form I-133 the location of the American Consulate as KRAKOW, Poland. Inasmuch as WARSAW, Poland is the only visa office in Poland, the visa petition has been changed to WARSAW, Poland.

Helen's Story

I was united in marriage to Carl Paul Staskus Jr. We had one beautiful daughter Jennifer who married Ryan. They have two children: Joseph and Julia my beloved grandchildren.

Unfortunately, Carl died at the age of 55. I miss him all the time.

Conclusion:

My family's journey took us through:

Four Continents: Europe, Asia, Africa, and North America.

Ten Countries: Poland, Soviet Union (including Republics of Uzbekistan and Turkmenistan), India, Iran, Tanganyika, (Father was in Iraq, Palestine, Egypt, and Italy), England and America.

We Traveled Through: plains, mountains, jungle, and deserts.

We Endured: severe temperatures of extreme cold (Siberia) to extreme heat (Uzbekistan, Iran, Iraq, and Tanganyika which was equatorial Africa.)

We Sailed on the: Gulf of Aden, Gulf of Oman, and the Persian Gulf.

We sailed on the: Arabian, Red, Caspian and Mediterranean Seas.

We sailed through: the Suez Canal, Strait of Gibraltar, and the English Channel.

We sailed on the: Indian and Atlantic Oceans.

Our difficult life's journey is perfectly summarized by Romans 8:18 which gives us hope in God's Eternal Word:

Romans 8:18 is authored by St. Paul and states: "For I consider that the sufferings of this present time are not worthy to be compared with the glory that is to be revealed in us."

May God the Father bless you through Jesus Christ my Lord and Savior!

Settling In:

My family was grateful to be in America starting a new life here.

An Alien has to be in this country 5 years to apply for citizenship and learning about this country. So, both Mom and Dad received their American Citizenship in 1957.

My heartfelt thanks to :

Adjunct Professor Nora Dusseault who found my publisher. Thank You Nora.

Also, to **Alan Lincourt** who immensely helped with the publication of this story.

Sincere thanks to you all!

Helen Rodzinka Staskus

References:

1. Mom's (Katarzyna) stories.
2. Zofia's recollections (on tape).
3. Zdzislaw's recollections (on tape) as well as numerous conversations.
4. Conversations with 1st Cousin Krystyna (Opalka) Szymanska.
5. Conversations with 2nd Cousin Dona (Opalka) Olejarczyk.
6. Conversations with Eugenia (Rosa) Frisco who was Zofia's friend.

Books:

1. "Stolen childhood" by Father Lucian Krolikowski,). F.M. Conv.
2. "Tulacze Dzieci/Exiled Children" Stories and Photographs were donated by Polish Exiles.
3. "Escape From Russia" by Stanley Opalka
4. Reader's Digest "Illustrated Stories of World War II"
5. The World Book Encyclopedia
6. Jana Parrelli Carstaedt who lives in New Mexico, a total stranger, is the daughter of a couple that I met briefly at my church in Herkimer, N.Y. around 2009. Jana, an expert in research, mailed me hundreds of pages of information pertinent to WWII and the effects it had on Poland and its people. Included was information on countries we lived in, treaties, copies of maps, photos, ship log records etc. I used much of this invaluable information.

With Gratitude I thank you Jana!

I extend my deep appreciation to my dear friend, **Karen Macrina**. She is the one who, back in 2009, encouraged me to write down my family's history.

Recently she again built up my confidence to expand the story. Karen devoted her time to typing, proof-reading, and helping me complete this project. I am completing seven folders of our family's story.

May our story bring Glory, Honor and Praise to Jesus Christ My Saviour who led us every step of the way.

1981

x Zofia   Zdsislaw   Janina   Antoni   Helena
x Sophie   Jess   Tony
x name changes after "naturalization"! Helen
        numbers show from Oldest onward!

Author with her husband and daughter.

Made in the USA
Columbia, SC
25 October 2021